MW00789654

THE POWER OF DIVINE TIMING

Dear
Colleen ♡
Hope Your Year is
filled with
Blessings

THE POWER OF DIVINE TIMING

The Secret to Success in Every Endeavor Is Timing

JOY YASCONE-ELMS

Waterside Productions

Copyright © 2022 by Joy Yascone-Elms

All rights reserved. This book or any portion thereof may not be reproduced or used in any manner whatsoever without the express written permission of the publisher except for the use of brief quotations in articles and book reviews.

ISBN-13: 978-1-958848-26-5 print edition
ISBN-13: 978-1-958848-27-2 e-book edition

Waterside Productions
2055 Oxford Ave
Cardiff, CA 92007
www.waterside.com

CONTENTS

ACKNOWLEDGEMENTS

I would like to dedicate this book to all of the people in my life who have nurtured me and my life force. If you're not included here and we've connected, you've shared a smile, kindness, friendship, or encouragement to me in any way, I graciously thank you. It takes a village – thank you for being part of mine. First to Waterside Productions, and my dear friends Bill and Gayle Gladstone. To my wonderful husband Thaddeus Bernard Elms, my mother "Glenda the good" ... Glenda Joy Yascone, my beloved brother-in-law, author, and poet, Bryan Santos Scichilone, my magical grandmother Hannah B. Akin, sister Love Ann Yascone, sister Faith Hope Yascone, Jon Katzman, Caroline Knop, co-founder and co-owner of *Sophisticated Living Magazine* Bridget Bailey Williams, owner of *Industry Magazine* Anthony, Chair of Holistic Health Georgian Court University Dr. Sachiko Komagata, Dr. Barbara Barr of Holistic Counseling Techniques. Also, to Private Label Lawyer and Dream Maker and good friend Suzi Hixon. Thanks to all of the friends and family who are mentioned here and who are not mentioned here that have been a source of light to me on my path. I love you, and thank you!

Preface – The Power of Divine Timing: Rags to Jupiter

My Introduction to Planet Jupiter!

I have always had a fascination with time, the ability to perceive things to come, mysticism, and astrology. The difference between astrology and intuitive ability is in astrology, we can pinpoint when things will potentially occur within a span of time. Generally, when a clairvoyant or intuitive looks at a situation, they can see who and what but generally not an exact calculation of a time when something will occur. I think this is simply because according to Einstein, time is really an illusion. It simply does not exist.

Yet, even as we embrace Einstein's theory of relativity, there is no past, present, and future – time is an illusion.

"People like us who believe in physics know that the distinction between past, present and future is only a stubbornly persistent illusion. Time, in other words, is an illusion."

— Albert Einstein

On Earth, however, we do observe time and have a desire to know when things will improve. *When will we meet the love of our life? When will we have the career of our desires and financial success?* We want to know when!

As we look at time on Earth, in this dimension, at least, time exists because we observe it. So, while having an Earth experience, we usually want to know when things will happen for us. It's just a part of human nature.

I've also always had an interest in what creates the fabric of someone's uniqueness and personality and how that is divined or designed by the stars and planets. People's unique strengths, weaknesses, talents, and gifts also can be determined and found in astrology.

It is with the birth chart – which I call the astrological fingerprint — that we can see these gifts and challenges within someone's personality as well as times of opportunity and challenge for current seasons and seasons to come within each person's unique astrological fingerprint or birth chart.

My grandmother Hannah would say I have always had this gift since I was little. My grandmother has since passed and was extremely gifted in clairvoyance and manifestation. She is full of God's grace, love, and power. She is pure magic. I say is and not was because energy never dies. We just transform, just as when you were a baby taking your first breath after leaving the familiar environment of your mother's womb. And you are born as you go through a tunnel toward a bright light. We are constantly transforming in this life and realm and in the next. So yes, she is and not was—she is. My grandmother would light up as I would write about topics when I was a child. She would delight in the information, and she knew it definitely came from a higher realm. She would say, "Joy, you have the gift!" —with an inference that she had the gift as well. I took it as a great compliment and the standard to live up to.

A great example of that is a play I wrote when I was a child called *Rags to Jupiter*. Not to get too much into the story, but the main character was a British child played by my sister Faith Hope

Yascone. The character she played spoke "cockney," the British slang language, and was living on the streets of London, rummaging for food because she did not understand or know her birthright. She was, in fact, royalty, but she didn't know it until she was rescued one day by the planet of benevolence, Jupiter!

At the time I wrote the play, I had no clue that Jupiter was the planet of benevolence and good fortune. I knew nothing of astrology as a child; the story just came to me because I loved to write. Music would come to me in the same way, like I was channeling it from the heavens. To get back to the story, this little girl was rescued by Jupiter and told of her birthright by the teacher planet that governs blessing seasons and good fortune — Jupiter! This is a fact in astrology, that Jupiter is the planet of good fortune, benevolence, and blessings, but I was unaware of it. That was a fictional play. However, that's exactly what Jupiter's influence can do!

In essence, Jupiter indicates in what part of life we will receive miracles. Jupiter in essence has the ability to light up an area of your life and "rescue" you, then you can also experience miracles and your birthright to master your unique and beautiful Universe. And the only thing required of you is that you give more intention and attention to your blessings than you do your challenges. When I was a child, I often feared studying the stars and planets as I was raised in the church. My grandfather was a Baptist minister, and I attended catholic school. However, in my studies, I noticed that even the wise men who were astrologers utilized the stars and signs to recognize the birth of Jesus. No matter what your religious beliefs are, the stars created by a magnificent creator or existing only in science show us a map of signs and things to come!

"And God said, Let there be lights in the firmament of the heaven to divide the day from the night; and let them be for signs, and for seasons, and for days, and years."

— Genesis 1:14

CHAPTER 1 – THE POWER OF DIVINE TIMING THROUGHOUT TIME

Right now, as I look at the upcoming months and where the planets are moving, my natural human instinct is to go into a place of concern where I see challenges for myself, my family, and close friends. However, the intention of this book is to do the exact opposite. The purpose of this book is to help each of us focus on what is feeding our lives. That is the blessings...the things going right! However, how do we find the things going right when the things going wrong hurt so bad?

The things going wrong cloud our vision with pain and with a feeling of no way out, when in reality, the way out is focusing on "the blessings" in our lives. In essence, it's what is feeding our lives as opposed to what is keeping us up late at night as we try to resolve it. In this book, I hope you will find a new and exciting way to use astrological data.

While Jupiter is the planet of blessings and good fortune — Saturn is the planet of challenges, limitations and lack. This book came about after 15 plus years of a painful "Saturn Season" in my Love, Fun, Marriage, and Commitment houses and the feeling that God had forgotten me. I kept having challenges in areas in which I wanted to experience the most joy in my life. I studied and practiced astrology for that 15-year period in order to understand my challenges. I later started my practice as an astrological life coach and my *The Power of Divine Timing* ™ coaching practice at The Wainwright House in Rye, New York while earning my master's degree in holistic health at Georgian Court University. I offered this simple yet counterintuitive approach to assist my clients on their life path.

I started to see my clients' lives change rapidly. We just rewired their thinking, thoughtfully examined their birth chart, and reconciled where the blessings were coming in so we could nurture the correct source of energy. For as we know, whatever you feed grows stronger! Feed the challenges, and they grow stronger and start to walk around like a giant monster. Feed the blessings, and they will grow and thrive as well.

The problem is that this is, in fact, very counterintuitive. If you have a problem, you think on it until you solve it, right? It works in math. However, in life and in utilizing *The Power of Divine Timing*, our goal is to shift intention away from what is challenging us and toward what is blessing our lives. We are usually taught not to focus on what is blessing our lives because it is simply not posing a problem. If it ain't broke, don't fix it… or, if it ain't broke, why focus on it? However, imagine if we were to focus on the parts of our lives that are feeding us and then nurture and feed those aspects! Would they not feed us more?

This is *The Power of Divine Timing* ™ — the technique that locates your specific, personal Universal blessings and challenges in real time and simply teaches you how to starve your challenges and nurture and grow your blessings!

The question then becomes, *what happens to something that starves?* It cannot exist without a source of energy feeding it. Simply put, this means you can starve your challenges to death until they have no power to survive and wreak havoc in your life. What I have intrinsically found is that when you focus on the blessings in your life, solutions for life's challenges can be found there. The question then becomes: *Where are my life's blessings? What is going to go right in my life? What is going right in my life now?* These can be hard questions when challenges are screeching loudly. However, a very easy answer is provided if we look to the placements of the stars and planets as they respond to our natal charts.

I can't see your entire chart while writing this book. However, by reading the chapters, *Nurture the Blessings – Divine Timing Blessing Seasons* and *Navigate the Challenges — Divine Timing Challenge Seasons,* and locating the dates of your sun sign and rising sign, you'll definitely be off to a good start!

Utilize *The Power of Divine Timing* to manifest the life you desire with Universal timing specific to your life path.

Chapter 2 – How to Utilize This Book

It's really quite easy. There are two divine timing season sections within *The Power of Divine Timing*, each with sign-by-sign dates illustrating when each sign will experience each divine timing season! The chapters *Nurture the Blessings – Divine Timing Blessing Seasons* and *Navigate the Challenges – Divine Timing Challenge Seasons* will get you started in navigating the challenges and nurturing the blessings.

It is imperative to be aware of what season you're in so you can nurture the correct source of energy at the correct time to manifest your ideal life. I've included Divine Timing Season dates for several years into the future so you can plan and practice your intention and focus in order to change your life! These divine timing seasons of blessings or challenges reveal specific timing for your Sun sign and rising sign, covering areas of life ranging from love and marriage, career and finance, to health and well-being, to name a few.

In the **Nurture the Blessings** chapters, you'll find your specific and personal divine timing blessing seasons and corresponding dates for all areas of life. These divine timing blessing seasons taught by Teacher Jupiter gift your life with good fortune and blessings during your personal and specific divine blessing seasons based on your Sun sign and rising sign. Dates for each sign to experience each divine season will be found at the beginning of each *Nurture the Blessings* and *Navigate the Challenges* chapter.

The other section, **Navigate the Challenges - Divine Timing Seasons,** also reveals sign-by-sign challenges in real time for the next several years.

Each divine timing season chapter focuses on current transits and movements and how they affect each astrological sign from the perspective of challenges and blessings. It also explains how to approach your current chart utilizing *The Power of Divine Timing*™ technique. You should read your Sun and rising sign dates for each blessing or challenge season. As you get familiar with this year's challenges and apparent Universal blessings, you can start to nurture the right source. As you nurture the correct source at the correct time, you will notice your life shifting, the challenges diminishing, and the blessings increasing. I have included exercises and suggestions for each of the astrological signs and transits to assist you in nurturing the right source.

Be sure to read your Sun and rising sign. Your rising sign or your ascendant is based on your birth time. Several free sites online offer this information, if you don't already have it. You can also have your chart prepared by an astrologer or an astrological intuitive, like myself. Please visit www.thepowerofdivinetiming.com for more information.

Even if you only have your Sun sign, this book will help you immensely. Its simplicity and methods have proven to help hundreds of my clients throughout the years. And now, I want to offer this simple yet effective method to my readers.

Okay, ready? Let's get started with finding the blessings then confirming the challenges so we can starve them ... and feed the right source. Ahhh ... that would be blessings!

CHAPTER 3 – THE POWER OF DIVINE TIMING: LOOKING AHEAD

As I look to the planets, each planet has a lesson plan designed for us, so I truly see the planets as teachers and astrology as an email from the Universe, or the heavens, if you will. Uranus is teaching us self-acceptance and originality; Saturn is teaching us discipline; Jupiter is teaching us benevolence and possibility; the Sun is teaching us manifestation; Neptune is teaching us spirituality; Venus is teaching us about beauty and what we truly value and how to get it. Meanwhile, Pluto teaches us about transformation, Mercury about communication, Mars assertiveness and survival, and the moon about intuition, and so on. We'll focus more on this topic a bit later in the book in *The Teachers* chapter.

Throughout the years as I have studied astrological data and have done hundreds of charts for clients, I have learned you can see everyone you know in your birth chart. The people you were born with and birth influences show up in your Natal chart, and the people, energies, and lessons along your path show up in the transits, which are the movement of the planets. There is a science to this Universe, no matter what your spiritual beliefs are, and while we only know in part and see in part, being aware of this and being in tune with the Universe can be very helpful along your path.

For the purposes of this book, we are looking at timing with the Universe and how it applies to what we would like to manifest, based on our birth data and the current timing and movement of the planets. In this book, we look at transits as seasons. We will learn what source to nurture at the correct time, based on your sun and rising sign, for you to achieve success in every area of life.

CHAPTER 4 – KEEP YOUR EYE ON THE PRIZE

What's not happening? What am I lacking? What's a problem in my life? Where is my life empty? And why is it so? These issues are signs of the human condition as we humans tend to be challenged or lack based by nature. We are so focused on the fear of lack as opposed to focusing on the expectation of blessings.

Saturn, the planet of challenges, is a teacher that likes to teach through a challenged-based reality. Saturn will reward you with hard work, responsibility, and discipline. All good things, right? Yes, excellent qualities … However, Saturn shines a light on what we are lacking in life so we can work to obtain it in the future when we have done the work and are ready! Jupiter, the planet of blessings, shines a light on what is blessing us now. However, we get so tied up with what we are lacking in life that we often feed the challenges and nurture them and ignore and starve the blessings.

You've heard the phrase, "Have an attitude of gratitude." That's all fine and dandy. I love the idea of a gratitude journal and all, but how can you be gracious if you can't see the blessings you're supposed to be grateful for? Indeed, sometimes we have starved the blessings so much, it's as if they do not exist, or they have simply withered and died. That's sad, right? Humans tend to naturally feed the wrong source. You may also know that whatever we feed, whatever we nurture, grows stronger. So, is it not wise to stop feeding the problem? A lot of times in life we are so focused on our issues or problems that they gain more strength and momentum than the blessings. *Why is this not happening? When will I meet that special someone? When will life get better? How can I see my life improve?*

What I've learned is that living in the moment and staying present in the present time will manifest your best life. You hear this time and time again from wise and prophetic teachers, "Live in the moment." However, how do you do that when you don't know what moment you're in or where to place your intention and energy?

We are taught to plan ahead and seek a vision for our desired future, and that is a good thing. Yet, it's important to not only be in the right now but to also know what that is and have the hope and knowledge to embrace it fully.

There is always a place in life where we feel we are experiencing great lack. Our desires are not being met, and somehow, we become consumed with the lack in our lives as opposed to the blessing. For instance, for many years, I really wanted great love in my life. I desired with all my heart to meet and marry my special someone. I often felt lonely, even in a crowded room.

I dated, I tried, and I failed with my choices; yet, all the while, I was having success in other areas of my life that I could not embrace due to my focus on what was lacking, a marriage partner. By being focused on the wrong thing at the wrong time, my career success, which was being greatly blessed at the time, was thwarted by my desire for true love.

I had so many magical things happening in my career, yet I could not embrace those things as I could only see the lack of not having the love of my life. I dated, and it always ended up the same – with my heart broken, sad, and alone. Little did I know I was going through divine timing challenge seasons with Master Teacher Saturn challenging me in my sectors of life governing love and marriage. I had a long divine challenge season of Saturn – which teaches through challenges – in my marriage, love, and romance sectors for over 15 years with my rising and Sun sign. However, during that time, I had amazing adventures with my family, which included my wonderful brother-in-law Bryan, my sisters, and our incredible Siberian Husky, Cheyenne, who would always accompany us. We traveled to Garden of the Gods, Sequoia National Park, Santa Barbara, California, and Vail, Colorado. Bryan and my sister Love, Bryan's wife, would organize these trips in a beautiful VW van. Bryan loved that VW Vanagon, and we had some wonderful times in nature. However, I was always distracted by what was lacking in my life – a marriage partner – as opposed to appreciating what was a blessing at the time – my family, travel, and, in essence, life.

While I was waiting for life to happen for me, it was happening. Now, I'm happily married and very much in love, and those moments I did not appreciate at the time are gone. Not to be a Debbie Downer, but those moments were special and rare, as Bryan later passed away tragically at a young age. I thought we had forever or at least more time than we were given with him. I'm so grateful for the wonderful times we had as a family; yet it is beyond comprehension. If I had been present, I could have lived more fully in the moment and really savored all of the blessings while I was going through a tough time in my love and marriage challenges brought on my planet of challenges Saturn.

Now that I am happily married, I long for those days again, but they are gone. Therefore, I'm writing this book to teach what I've learned – how to see the good in life in the present and how to maximize your blessings in the moment, utilizing astrological data and divine timing seasons. With this book, you'll not only learn the methodology of *The Power of Divine Timing* but also where the blessings and challenges are coming into your life for the next 12-year divine season, all specific to you. You will also learn where you should place your intention and focus. Through giving you this knowledge and the methodology behind it, I hope to help you nurture the right source at the right time—to live fully in the moment and have an attitude of gratitude as you nurture the blessings and bring them back to life.

CHAPTER 5 – LACK VERSUS GRATITUDE

Saturn, who governs over the divine timing challenge seasons, teaches with a challenged-based reality, so you must prove you're ready for rewards with discipline and responsibility. Saturn will make you desire something that you are perhaps truly not ready for, or it is not ready for you. You can bet when you're experiencing Divine Timing Challenge Season Two, which is by definition a transit or season of Saturn to your second house of earned income, you'll feel a sense of lack in regard to money.

You'll desire a new job. You'll be unhappy with how you are earning an income. In essence, a Saturn-based perception of reality would have you start focusing on that lack of earned income. Although, at the time—hypothetically, for example— you are experiencing Divine Timing Blessing Season Nine in which Jupiter, the planet of blessings, is transiting your ninth house or sector of higher education. If you focus on the topic of higher education or perhaps a job that's covered in this area of life such as publishing, teaching, or broadcasting, you could prevail in pretty much every area of life.

Saturn, the planet of challenges, does not hate you or want you to suffer. Saturn just wants you to be disciplined and responsible in your approach or otherwise suffer. Saturn will taunt you by shining the light on what is lacking in your life, so you commit to the hard work of getting it. If you rush in before you are ready with an approach that is not structured or disciplined, Saturn will rip the rug right out from underneath you. That's why a Saturn season denotes challenges, because we human beings generally want what we feel we can't have or, in this case, what we don't have yet!

A good example of this is my Capricorn friend; we'll call her Linda. She and her husband, William, came into town, looking to relocate from Wisconsin to North Carolina. This was such exciting news for me as I moved to North Carolina after my husband's job relocated us there, and I was friendless. My friend Linda is a Capricorn, so she represents Saturn, the planet of lessons through discipline, challenges, diligence, and hard work. Linda embodies all of these qualities. She is a hardworking doctor of pharmacy. She is financially stable and very disciplined in her approach to life and work. She is the perfect representation of Saturn as Saturn is the natural ruler of Capricorn. William and Linda made life exciting. We all went out together, enjoying live music, dinners out, and friendship—something I was greatly missing in my life.

We also enjoyed touring houses because they were looking for their new home in the triangle area of Raleigh, Durham, and Chapel Hill. Our friends would be relocating to our neck of the woods within a year or less. How exciting! I love looking at homes—new, old, beach, urban, Home Fairs, HGTV, Chip and Joanna Gaines ... you've got it! My mom also happens to be an amazing interior designer. This search with William and Linda stirred my desire to own my own special home. I had always dreamt of having a sweet bungalow when my husband and I married. I love history, charm, and a mid-size, spacious-but-manageable home. When my husband and I married, he picked out our residence. It was a suburban home built in the 1980s, around 3,500 plus square feet, and full of carpet and brass. It was a beautiful dream home, complete with a saltwater pool, outdoor kitchen, and walkout basement. I agreed to get the home because my husband had reluctantly agreed to move to Kentucky when he was offered a job with a San Francisco-based tech company that had recently relocated to my hometown of Louisville. I agreed that if he moved to Kentucky, he got to pick out the house. We purchased the home, but I never felt a connection or a true liking for that house at all. It was devoid of what I craved ... charm, character, and my spirit.

William and Linda's search reminded me how much I wanted a home that I loved with a private backyard for myself and our dog—a place that is ours.

Saturn shined a light on what I was lacking. We had sold our 1980s suburban home in Kentucky and were renting a nice yet small, two-bedroom condo. It was in a bustling community that had several life advantages and conveniences, but the condo was a bit too cramped for our needs at the time with my stepdaughter (we both prefer the term "bonus daughter") living with us full time and our 62-pound Goldendoodle. He was fine, happy, and adjusted, but I felt cramped and trapped in our small condo with no private backyard and a huge dog.

As my friends searched for and found their home, I was so excited for them. Meanwhile, had I stayed present in the moment, there were so many other places in life that were offering me blessings – my career, job, etc. But I could only see what was lacking in life – I had no home, no yard, and lived in a small, cramped condo with my bonus daughter and dog. To reiterate the point, when I offered a prayer for my Capricorn friend and her husband that everything would go smooth and easy with the closing of the contract on their home, my friend Linda responded as only a Saturn-governed Capricorn can, "Nothing smooth or easy is appreciated." Case in point! Saturn believes you must work hard to get rewarded, and, might I add, there is nothing wrong with hard work.

I was hosting Saturn in my "house of home"or area of my chart governing home during that time, and as I have studied the planets and their transits, Saturn's job is really not to make us miserable. Saturn's job is to show us what is lacking in life, so we get up and make it happen for ourselves. Saturn wants us to be disciplined in our approach and work hard to make our dreams and desires happen. The only problem for me was, it was not my time to purchase a house yet. We were still very unsettled as to where we wanted to put roots down. If we would have purchased where I originally wanted to purchase, my drive to the office would have been treacherous. We still had another 10 months left on our lease at our small condo, and I was due to get my real estate license in a few months, which would credit us the realtor's commission toward the purchase of our home.

On top of that, we were not sure where we really wanted to live. However, I could not help but be completely consumed with the possibility of living in a nice, charming, full-of-light home that I liked or potentially loved! However, when working with a Saturn season like this one I had with my house of home and real estate, it's best to wait and work from other areas of blessing, recognizing where the planet of blessings and benevolence, Jupiter, is shining a light, if you're paying attention … and it was my career.

The divine time was right to work on my career and just spruce up my small condo until the time was right to purchase. My schedule at work was to travel Monday and Tuesday, arriving home early evening on Wednesday anyway, so it would work out perfectly to stay in our small yet charming Airbnb property in the beach town of Wilmington, a place my husband truly loves, as the water is a place, we both find peace and solitude. Timing is everything, as they say … and it's so true that staying in the moment you are in, the current moment, can get you to your dream house, dream life, and dream goals, but only with the right focus at the right time and a dose of grace and gratitude.

Chapter 6 – Blessings Versus Challenges in Their Truest Form

Divine blessing seasons are governed by Master Teacher Jupiter, and there's only one possibility – anything is possible! Jupiter doesn't have to stop and give a speech or convince anyone. Jupiter just makes it happen without wasting any time. How marvelous! Jupiter, planet of "go big or go home" as he travels through the constellations and various star signs of the Zodiac, requires each sign to carry out his specific blessing and benevolence orders. When you read the *Nurture the Blessings – Divine Timing Blessing Seasons* chapter or *Navigate the Challenges – Divine Timing Challenge Seasons* chapter, be sure to read all twelve blessing seasons and all twelve challenge seasons and note the dates you will experience each blessing or challenge season. Note the dates for each season by looking up your Sun sign and rising sign dates for both.

These sign-by-sign divine timing blessing season dates and divine timing challenge season dates are at the start of each of the twelve chapters. When experiencing a divine challenge season, you'll want to adjust and learn from it while starving that challenge as much as possible and nurturing your blessing season instead. It's not that we don't need to acknowledge our challenges. We do, but we also need to nourish our blessings as our challenges are being overfed and our blessings are being starved.

In noting the different schools of thought from Saturn, teacher of the divine challenge seasons, and Jupiter, teacher of divine blessing seasons, when it comes down to it, these two planets just believe in two different schools of thought. Saturn believes that only hard work deserves a reward, and if you pursue something without being properly prepared, worthy, or ready, Saturn will inflict harsh consequences. Teacher Jupiter believes in teaching divine blessings seasons through possibility and benevolence. Jupiter is where you focus and where you stay in the moment of life's current blessings.

During Teacher Saturn's divine timing challenge seasons or when you experience a feeling of lack or an unfulfilled desire or stress. It's usually an area of life that will require much of you and is generally riddled with trials and challenges until you've satisfied Teacher Saturn in a divine challenge season that you've done the hard work to deserve the desired reward. It is my aim with this book to teach you how to nurture the correct source or blessing season at the right time. That would be where you are most fortunate in the here and now. This is how you live in gratitude and the moment.

Chapter 7 – Marriage, Career, Love, Financial Success: "Not Now" Does Not Mean "Not Ever"

One thing I really love about the study of the movement of the planets and how they affect us on Earth is that it offers hope the tide will change. Sometimes in life, it feels like nothing will ever work out. You'll never meet "the one," you'll never get better, you'll never lose weight, or you'll never be successful. However, the study of astrology is the study of the movement of the planets, through the constellations, or heavens, and how that affects us on Earth. When I studied astrology for that 15-year period of divine timing challenges in my love and marriage sectors of life, I learned by observation and studying past events during a particular divine season or transit that this movement is like a continuum of the planets playing musical chairs. Life is consistently moving forward, even if we choose to stay stuck.

While learning about time through astrology and manifestation, we can see that life will inevitably change. There will be a time for marriage, there will be a time for career, and there is a time for quiet contemplation. There are times when it is good to invest in real estate, and there are times when it is good to invest in the stock market. I feel that for those of us who need a little bit of hope along the way, astrology teaches us that nothing stays the same forever.

There is always hope! The Universe provides that, so it's about time for us to recognize it and nurture the blessings. It is the human condition to give our challenges too much attention and intention.

I like to use astrology as a tool for manifesting an amazing life. While astrological data forecasts a potential future, if used properly, it can be a gift to stay very present in the moment. For instance, suppose you know you will be entering into a season of divine challenges impacting your house or sector of life in marriage and partnerships at this time. You can lean into that, realizing it's a place you need to focus on for the future. However, Jupiter shows us where we are right now—where we can experience the Irish Blessing, going with the tide instead of against it. It's not as if you should not desire what Saturn is pointing out that you lack. Instead, you should say, "Great, that's something I know I want for my future. However, today I'll focus on where Jupiter is shining the light of grace."

The Power of Divine Timing should be utilized to focus on the divine timing blessing season Teacher Jupiter is shining a light on, representing blessings and grace, as opposed to the sector of life that is being challenged by a divine season of Teacher Saturn. This is the way to live fully in the moment while knowing what you desire can be obtained and manifested in due season. This method nurtures appreciation and gratitude as we can stay present and gracious in the current moment. This is such a smart way to live and manifest a happy life that is moving forward. I try to master it daily as this counterintuitive approach takes practice. Now, let's get started!

"It's not that we don't need to acknowledge our challenges. We do, but we also need to nourish our blessings as our challenges are being overfed and our blessings are being starved."

– Joy Yascone-Elms

CHAPTER 8 – WAITING FOR THE TIDE TO CHANGE VERSUS LIVING IN THE MOMENT

In life, it may often feel like we're waiting for the tide to change as opposed to going with the flow. We are waiting for the next big promotion, the next big deal, a marriage partner or true love, to get fit, healthy or to simply be happy.

All of these things are important aspects of life. I feel having love in your life is definitely a beautiful thing. Being successful and having a great win is worthy of celebration. Having a beautiful financial picture can bless your family and your offspring for years to come. It is that hope of future blessings – that hope of change – that keeps us alive many times.

It makes life worth the fight to have hope and a plan for the future. These are all wonderful things. And there is a season for all of these things to happen for you within divine timing, if you learn to go with the flow and wisdom of the stars to understand the natural flow of abundance of the Universe.

As we have spoken about in other sections of this book, we place our intention where we are feeling a sense of lack in our lives. As we work or wait for the tide to change, many times we miss out on the blessings that are right at our doorstep, calling out for our intention and energy ever so softly to place intention there as opposed to our place of challenge or where we feel we're experiencing much lack.

Lack can be a great thing as it can create a need or the knowledge of a need to work to create what is missing in life. However, most of us become obsessed with what is lacking in our lives and therefore miss the area of life that has the most ease. This leads to missing an area of blessing at the current moment because our mind can only focus on what is missing or lacking in our lives.

This thought process most definitely takes us out of the moment and out of the gratitude for the blessings we currently have, and we actually need to manifest what is lacking. This is why I'll reference the Irish Blessing many times when you hear me speak or throughout this book. We want to go with the flow with the wind at our back and the roads rising up to meet us. In order for that to happen, we must take account of our current blessings and not just have grace and gratitude for them. We need to experience them fully and live them fully for it is from that area of life in which we are experiencing blessings that we create what is lacking.

"May the road rise up to meet you.
May the wind be always at your back.
May the sun shine warm upon your face,
And the rains fall soft upon your fields.
And until we meet again,
May God hold you in the palm of His hand."

— An Irish Blessing

CHAPTER 9 – "IF IT AIN'T BROKE, DON'T FIX IT!"

There's an age-old antidote or belief that "If it ain't broke, don't fix it!" This basically means if it's not posing a problem, then don't give it any intention or energy. If it's working, then leave it alone. However, this thought process is exactly what gets us in trouble in our divine blessing seasons and leads to only focusing on the challenges that are vying for our attention.

"If it ain't broke, don't fix it!" basically gives the impression that if it's not screaming for attention or posing a problem, there is no need to nurture it. And this can't be further from the truth. This thought process can lead to missing out on memories with your family, missing out on nurturing the current moment and relationships, and missing out on career opportunities and blessings that have been gifted to you in a specific divine blessing season. And once you miss a blessing season, it takes 12 years to experience a return to that sector of life to deliver a similar divine blessing season.

That's why it's so important to be present in the moment and nurture the things that "ain't broke" – the things that are working for you, the blessings. Never take those moments or seasons for granted.

By only focusing on what's broken — our challenges, we essentially starve our blessings and nurture our challenges when it should be the other way around. We should clearly be nurturing the aspects of life that are nurturing and feeding us.

That is a big purpose of this book – to help you locate your blessings in real time so you can nurture the right source of energy, thereby creating desired results in every area of your life. It's admitted that this approach is very counterintuitive. However, this approach leads to creating the most sustainable results to build the life of your dreams.

It's the most efficient way to utilize astrology and astrological data for manifestation!

Chapter 10 – The Teachers

The Planets are Like Professors at a Divine University - Life

We look to the stars and the planets and how they transit or "travel" our natural assigned traits, in essence, our natal chart. Our natal chart, also referred to as our birth chart, is established by the exact time and place we were born and when we take our first breath incarnating on Earth. We can see that each planet is teaching a subject and helping us hone those specific skills. Our birth chart is as individual as a fingerprint and interacts with the current movement of the planets or transits, creating potential outcomes based on our choices.

Our birth chart is fixed and established at our birth. Our fixed birth chart and placements of our ascendant, Sun, Moon, Venus, Mars, Mercury, Jupiter, Saturn, Uranus, Neptune and Pluto are all based on birthdate, birth time, and birth location, including longitude and latitude, to create this astrological fingerprint of our unique individual birth charts. These unique and individualized charts show our strengths, weaknesses, natural gifts, and talents and establish the points and times in which certain events could occur in our lives.

The transits of the planets through the constellations along with our birth chart establish how the current movement of the planets will affect us. To establish the events within an "Earth" timeline in astrology and astrological wisdom, our ascendant starts the moment we take our first breath. The moment we are born and start to breathe on our own. This chosen time to incarnate on Earth establishes and sets up your birth chart and when events may impact you. With this knowledge, we can fully witness the picture of each planet and the lessons they are teaching us. The planets are like teachers or professors of beauty and divinity at a divine university which is life. Each planet, I believe, teaches us a different lesson.

The Sun governs over Leo and teaches us manifestation and the art of creation and creativity, also teaching us to have a child-like sense of wonder and the ability to create and give life. The Sun's movements also create our Sun signs for without the Sun, there is no life or procreation. **The Moon** governs over Cancer and teaches us to listen to our inner self and our intuition and make wise choices and decisions. The Moon is intuitive, teaching us to mind our moods and inner feelings and listen to our inner guidance. **Mercury** governs over Gemini and Virgo and teaches us to communicate, share ideas, and negotiate. Teacher Mercury governs over all forms of communication. Mercury also teaches us the importance and power of excellent communication.

Venus governs over Taurus and Libra and teaches us what we value and what matters most to us; for instance, a beloved child could hold more value to you than the wealth of many nations. **Mars** governs over Aries and teaches us to be assertive and about passion. *Mars* also teaches us to fight for what we believe in and to be a force of power – picture Sparta 300, charging forward with the will to win.

Master Teacher Jupiter governs over Sagittarius, and all blessing seasons. Jupiter teaches us about receiving unconditional benevolence and the gift of being benevolent to others. It also teaches us that anything is possible and there is good and kindness in the world. We can learn the power of miracles that is available to us and the grace and gift of how it feels to receive and give kindness and unconditional love to everyone. That grace is a gift that can't be earned; however, you have to make your intentions known and nurture your belief. Master Teacher Jupiter teaches the twelve blessing seasons in the Nurture the Blessings seasons chapters. Jupiter believes that through benevolence, grace, and good fortune, we as students learn that nothing is impossible, and everything is possible. Jupiter teaches us about faith, hope, and endless possibility.

Master Teacher Saturn, the ruler of Capricorn, teaches us about responsibility and due process and following the rules, whether that's the scientific rules of gravity or the rules of baking a cake to create success. As baking is very scientific, if you miss baking powder, baking soda, or a certain number of eggs, or any other necessary ingredients, the chemistry of the recipe won't work. So is it with Saturn. This planet wants you to follow the rules to create success in any endeavor. You must prove to Saturn that you have completed all of the necessary steps before receiving any reward.

Saturn is a master teacher and the professor that teaches the 12 divine timing challenge seasons which you can find in the Navigate the Challenges chapter. Saturn believes we should learn that if we touch the fire when it is hot, we get burnt. Saturn believes we must develop resilience in the testing of our responsibilities, the ability to sacrifice, and the wherewithal to go through challenges and/ or pain to truly learn in a divine challenge season. Again, Saturn believes that we learn through lack and challenge. When you get to the divine timing challenge seasons chapter, you can locate the dates of your Sun and corresponding Sun sign of each divine timing challenge season and notate what challenge you may experience in a particular season. Remember, we will acknowledge the challenges while shifting more energy to Jupiter.

Uranus, ruler of Aquarius, teaches us how to be original, how to break the rules, and how to be affirmative of our own uniqueness without the need of someone else's approval.

Pluto, Scorpio's governing planet, teaches us about re-creation – that we can always bounce back, being resilient and coming back to life after a death or a figurative death such as a painful break up or career loss. Pluto teaches us the power of recreation, like the Phoenix rising from the ashes.

And finally, **Neptune**, ruler of Pisces, teaches us that art and inspiration is in everything, and that spirituality is very different from religion. Neptune is teaching us to live in the moment and be fully present. Neptune's teachings are an accumulation of all the life lessons in one.

When we understand that life is like a divine school and the planets are our teachers, we can experience each divine timing season. Whether it is a divine blessing season or a divine challenge season, manifest greater results toward your dreams and goals by nurturing the correct source of energy at the correct time.

"The planets are not them — they are us."

— Joy Yascone-Elms

Chapter 11 – Two Parenting Styles: Blessings Versus Challenges, Saturn Versus Jupiter

Saturn and Jupiter are master teachers, teaching us at different seasons in our lives. Jupiter's class and divine season lasts approximately 12 months, and Saturn's divine challenge season class lasts 2½-3 years. All of the planets are teaching us lessons. However, I would say Saturn and Jupiter teach us not only the most polarizing lessons but also teach us similar lessons with different approaches.

In our manifestations of goals and dreams in life, it is the placement of these two planets that makes the most impact. Saturn's teaching style is through a challenged-based reality and through shining a light on what we are lacking. Saturn highlights what we are currently missing in life and believes no one appreciates that which comes easily. If you want to be fit and healthy, Saturn wants to see you put in the effort. Take preventative measures and work out, have a fitness routine, eat healthy, and follow the methods and habits that create good health. Saturn wants methods and order. This planet that teaches with a lack-based reality wants to note that if you want a marriage partner, you are ready for the challenge and understand the sacrifices you need to make, and you are fully prepared for that challenge and gift.

Saturn appreciates following processes and procedures and wants us to do things from start to finish in a logical and correct way in order to create desired results. Saturn's approach is difficult and challenging but absolutely necessary. Without Saturn's lessons, we wouldn't appreciate the blessing of finding a special someone, a life mate, or a partner. We would think it was easy and partnerships are a dime a dozen. However, with Saturn's influence or transit in this sector of life ruling marriage and partnerships (experienced in this book as Divine Timing Lesson Seven), we get to experience the pain, loneliness, and alienation of this lesson. Saturn, in essence, gifts us with the pain of not having a partner or an equal counterpart so that when we are in that divine blessing season and "the one" does come along, we respect the partnership and the value it holds for our lives.

The best way to work with these challenging points and challenging lessons is to acknowledge where you're experiencing lack. However, focus and nurture the aspects of your life that are currently experiencing the blessings or good fortune of the placements of Jupiter.

Recognize the challenge and the feelings of lack, but put much of your energy into where you are experiencing ease in life at the current moment. That is the placement of Jupiter. You will find sign-by-sign timing on these periods of opportunity in the Nurture the Blessing section of this book.

Jupiter likes to teach through a benevolent reality. Jupiter, as a master teacher planet, wants everyone to have opportunities for blessings in every area of life. Jupiter, the planet of good fortune and the planet of blessings, travels through each sign and stays for the time span of 12 months. Each sign, constellation and/or sector "house" represents a different area of life for us, based on our sun sign and rising sign.

Jupiter moves more quickly than Saturn. Saturn spends 2½-3 years in each sign or sector of life, representing challenges and lack. Jupiter speaks through giving gifts. If you're not paying attention to the blessing period or the time, you're in with Jupiter, you can completely miss it, and that would be a tragedy.

This is where grace and gratitude come in. With Jupiter's benevolence and kindness, we are gifted with Twelve Seasons of Blessings with opportunities for the repeat of a blessing season every 12 years.

Jupiter gives with equal opportunity of blessings for each sign for a different focus or area of life. So, no matter what time or season you're in or what challenges, you can be assured things will get better as the planets keep moving. Saturn will move out of a challenging angle in your chart eventually, and Jupiter, the planet of blessings and good fortune, will move into that sector of life eventually. As such, we each have the opportunity for the gifts of Jupiter and the blessings of Jupiter in sectors of life that previously endured challenges. It's just imperative to learn how to utilize these patterns and periods of opportunity.

Everyone has a season of blessings in the sector of life concerning love and marriage, everyone has a season of blessings in the sector of life of health and wellness, and everyone has a season of blessings in the area of career and finance. In addition, everyone has the blessings of a season of protection over home and parents. The problem is when we are gifted with the divine blessing seasons, we often don't notice it because the squeaky wheel gets the grease.

Planet Jupiter, the planet of blessing seasons, is not loud nor squeaky. It is generous – go big or go home. Yet it is also soft and nurturing and wants you to utilize the areas of opportunity that are being presented to you. It also wants you to sit up and take notice. Change your thinking and start nurturing the blessings.

Chapter 12 – Seasons Change

The great thing about seasons is they change.

We have so many seasons in life, and a lot of times, when going through a rough or challenging season, it may feel as if it will never end. However, noting that seasons change, we can be assured that this will not be the case. However, in the thick of it, it definitely appears to be something that will last forever.

A blessing season has a duration as well as a challenge season. The thing I love about seasons, particularly divine seasons, is that they always change. Seasons never stay the same forever—that's important to note as we go through difficult challenges. Challenges are given different seasons for different sectors of our life. And our results with challenges or with a challenging season is all in how we approach it. Being aware of your seasons can help you to live with the wind at your back and the roads rising up to meet you. If you're aware of what season you are in, it can help you stay in the moment, realizing that if it's a season of divine blessing, you must treasure the moment because even fruitful blessing seasons shift and change.

If you are in a stressful challenge season – which is also a divine season but challenging — it's a wonderful feeling to know that the season will eventually change as well because seasons are consistent in that they always change.

In *The Power of Divine Timing*, we refer to the stars and transits of planets as seasons.

The outer planets like Uranus, Pluto, and Neptune have a huge effect on our lives but more in a generational way. Their lessons are taught over much longer periods of time. The season-makers that establish these seasons of blessings or challenges are Master Teacher Saturn and Master Teacher Jupiter. These planetary teachers have a way of approaching each area of our chart in seasons, like divine lesson plans. You can truly start to walk with the wind at your back and the road rising up to meet you with the understanding that there will be a season for everything under the sun and there will be a time when you have the opportunities you feel you are lacking. However, to be in complete flow with the Universe, we must take account of our blessings and nurture and feed them, so our seasons are not fraught with challenges but the blessings that manifest the gifts we so desire.

"To everything there is a season, and a time for every purpose under the heavens."

— Ecclesiastes 3:1

Chapter 13 – The Power of Divine Timing: Nurture the Twelve Divine Blessing Seasons

There are certain seasons of our life that are advantageous for blessings and good fortune. Yet many times, we are so focused on what is not occurring in our life that we cannot fully participate in the seasons of blessing at hand. That is the intention of this book – to help you live in the moment and manifest your greatest dreams and intentions, utilizing *The Power of Divine Timing* to help you nurture the correct source of energy at the correct time. The correct time is found in your divine timing blessing seasons so you can manifest your desired intentions while staying present in the moment of your current blessing season. You may notice I repeat and reiterate a lot during this book as I believe repetition is the mastery of skill.

When we are in a divine timing blessing season, it's imperative that we really stay present in the moment because seasons change, and we can miss a blessing season very quickly. Challenge seasons and challenge lessons last longer than specific divine blessing seasons because the planet that teaches divine blessing seasons — Jupiter – blesses one area of our life for a duration of only 12 months. If we are distracted by the lessons of Teacher Saturn as we navigate the challenges, we can miss an entire blessing season and the needed seeds to create and grow exactly what we are lacking.

A divine timing blessing season will last only 12 months, while a divine timing challenge season taught by Teacher Saturn lasts 2½-3 years in a particular challenge season of our life. Perhaps that is why challenge seasons tend to speak so loudly because they simply last longer. We have grown so accustomed to the long challenge season that when the blessing comes in, we are too distracted to take notice. However, blessing seasons require that we be aware of them while we have them so we can plant seeds, nurture them, and see them grow over the next 12-year cycle until Teacher Jupiter again gifts us with the same divine blessing season in 12 years. Divine blessing seasons repeat every 12 years. In this chapter, Nurture the Blessings – Divine Blessing Seasons One through Twelve, you'll get to know firsthand by your sun sign, rising sign, and the corresponding dates as to when you'll be experiencing each divine timing blessing season. At the end of each Divine Timing Blessing Season One through Twelve, there is a focus section. This is the divine blessing season you want to put your intention and focus on during the duration of that particular season. To experience the best results, take notes and highlight seasons of blessings and focus so you can put into practice nurturing the correct source of energy at the correct time.

"Repetition is the mother of learning, the father of action, which makes it the architect of accomplishment."

- Zig Ziglar

<u>Nurture the Blessings</u>

Divine Timing Blessing – Season One

You Are Lady Luck –
"One Miracle At a Time Please."

Divine Time You Are in Now

Aries (March 21 - April 19)
You will experience Divine Timing Blessing Season One during this time.

May 10, 2022, to October 28, 2022
December 20, 2022, to May 16, 2023
April 21, 2034, to April 29, 2035

Taurus (April 20 - May 20)
You will experience Divine Timing Blessing Season One during this time.

May 16, 2023, to May 25, 2024
April 29, 2035, to May 9, 2036
April 13, 2047, to April 22, 2048

Gemini (May 21 - June 20)
You will experience Divine Timing Blessing Season One during this time.

May 25, 2024, to June 9, 2025
May 9, 2036, to May 23, 2037
April 22, 2048, to September 23, 2048
November 12, 2048, to May 5, 2049

Cancer (June 21 - July 22)
You will experience Divine Timing Blessing Season One during this time.

June 9, 2025, to June 30, 2026
May 23, 2037, to June 12, 2038
September 23, 2048, to November 12, 2048
May 5, 2049, to September 27, 2049

Leo (July 23 - August 22)
You will experience Divine Timing Blessing Season One during this time.
June 30, 2026, to July 26, 2027
June 12, 2038, to November 16, 2038
January 16, 2039, to July 7, 2039

Virgo (August 23 - September 22)
You will experience Divine Timing Blessing Season One during this time.
July 26, 2027, to August 24, 2028
November 16, 2038, to January 16, 2039
July 7, 2039, to December 12, 2039
February 20, 2040, to August 5, 2040

Libra (September 23 - October 22)
You will experience Divine Timing Blessing Season One during this time.
August 24, 2028, to September 24, 2029
December 12, 2039, to February 20, 2040
August 5, 2040, to January 11, 2041
March 20, 2041, to September 5, 2041

Scorpio (October 23 - November 21)
You will experience Divine Timing Blessing Season One during this time.
September 24, 2029, to October 22, 2030
January 11, 2041, to March 20, 2041
September 5, 2041, to February 8, 2042
April 24, 2042, to October 4, 2042

Sagittarius (November 22 - December 21)
You will experience Divine Timing Blessing Season One during this time.

October 22, 2030, to November 15, 2031

February 8, 2042, to April 24, 2042

October 4, 2043, to June 9, 2043

Capricorn (December 22 - January 19)
You will experience Divine Timing Blessing Season One during this time.

November 15, 2031, to April 11, 2032

June 26, 2032, to November 29, 2032

March 1, 2043, to June 9, 2043

October 26, 2043, to March 15, 2044

August 9, 2044, to November 4, 2044

Aquarius (January 20 - February 18)
You will experience Divine Timing Blessing Season One during this time.

December 19, 2020, to May 13, 2021

July 28, 2021, to December 28, 2021

April 11, 2032, to June 26, 2032

November 29, 2032, to April 14, 2033

September 12, 2033, to December 1, 2033

March 15, 2044, to August 9, 2044

Pisces (February 19 - March 20)
You will experience Divine Timing Blessing Season One during this time.

May 13, 2021, to July 28, 2021

December 28, 2021, to May 10, 2022

October 28, 2022, to December 20, 2022

April 14, 2033, to September 12, 2033

December 1, 2033, to April 21, 2034

Nurture the Blessings
Divine Timing Blessing –
Season One

When you're experiencing Divine Timing Blessings Season One, life is about to get much more interesting! This is the time you are immensely blessed by the power and luck of planet Jupiter! Not only is it a lucky time when you can manifest just about anything, it's also the time in which you become the power of Jupiter to others. During this season, you will represent benevolence and good fortune to others, but this will also equal benevolence and good fortune for you.

I experienced this blessing phenomenon when I was going off to grad school to get my master's degree in holistic health in New Jersey. At the time, I didn't have a lot of money. However, I was determined to go and so excited to go to graduate school at Georgian Court University, which felt like being at Hogwarts. Jupiter was in Aquarius at the time, and I had no idea of the blessings that would be before me. Jupiter in Aquarius had so many surprises for me, and the very people who were the biggest blessings to me were Aquarians. Hence, they became Jupiter.

On the long drive to graduate school, my mom and sisters accompanied me as I packed up the car on a whim after getting a notice that I was accepted into the graduate program which started in a week. I was in for a big surprise when I got there. The campus was over 156 acres and was magical; it was like going back in time. It was historic, mystical, and beautiful, and I was pleasantly shocked and beyond surprised. However, Georgian Court was in Lakewood, New Jersey. While it had the most beautiful and magical campus I've ever seen, it wasn't really a thriving community to live in. At the time, we were looking for hotels to stay in, and everything was booked around the area. The only thing I could find was roughly 25 minutes away in a town called Red Bank, New Jersey. We booked a room at the courtyard as it was the only thing available in the entire area for some reason.

What a strike of luck that was! Red Bank was a happening town that was the yin to the yang of the peacefulness of Georgian Court University. It had a Jersey Shore attitude with high fashion and exotic cars, Lamborghini, Versace, beautiful people, and a thriving town. This was such a surprise, and of course, Jupiter being in Aquarius planet Uranus (which hopefully you read about in The Teachers section) loves to shock and surprise, and I was getting wonderful Jupiter blessing surprises everywhere!

My mom, sisters, and I went for some coffee at the local coffee shop, knowing I needed to find a place to live right away. Only undergraduate students could stay on campus, not graduate students. We walked into the coffee shop and asked around, but no one seemed to know of anything available. We were about to leave the coffee shop when something told me to turn around and look, and I saw a "For Rent" sign on the back of the door of the coffee shop. I immediately proceeded to call the number. When the owner answered the phone, little did I know that this too would be a life-changing moment. "Hello," I said, "I'm here to go to graduate school, and I would love to rent your loft available above the coffee shop." A male voice on the other side of the phone said, "I'm around the corner. I'm the owner. It's absolutely beautiful. You'll love it! When you walk right out your front door, you're in the action with all the shops and dining. It has high ceilings and is an open loft – only $1,800 a month." When he met me at the coffee shop in the building he owned, we talked and shared laughs. I told him I was not sure I could afford the $1,800 a month while in graduate school. We agreed that it might not work out, but I'd save his number.

My mom asked him where we should go to dinner, and he told us about the Italian restaurant across the street. That evening, we took his advice, and it was wonderful! None other than Anthony, the building and loft owner showed up! We had a wonderful conversation, laughed, and enjoyed a wonderful evening. It was complete synchronicity and magic. The next thing I knew, Anthony offered me a job to help pay for the loft while I was working at his designer store and attending grad school. Everything worked out. I even had a job working at grad school because the store was open until 11 p.m. I was able to do both and was very successful in school and at work.

Oh, yes, and I forgot to say I have an Aquarius rising, and while it may appear that Anthony was only helping me out, his benevolence to me was an amazing decision. I became his top salesperson, selling millions of dollars' worth of merchandise and making him a lot of money.

I share this story to say that many times when you become Jupiter, in essence benevolence and good fortune, you're actually inviting blessings into your life that you would never imagine. Get ready for your time of Blessings Season One. I used the word season because seasons change, and that is exactly what happens within the context of divine timing. We have a season for everything under the sun, and this is your season to not only become benevolent and offer good fortune for others but also for yourself. When you are in Divine Timing Blessing Season One, it's imperative not to rest on your past accomplishments. You need to really utilize the time of blessings when you have the wind at your back to create miracles which is what you have the power to do at this time!

When you're experiencing Blessing Season One, it can be healing for your mind, body, and spirit. If you need help healing your physical body, Jupiter indicates miracles here, particularly when you're experiencing Divine Blessing Season One on your sun sign which governs your vitality. You can experience Blessing Season One impacting your rising/ascendant sign or on your Sun. Either way, this time is a time you might imagine sitting with kings and queens and they ask you what you would like to manifest, and you simply must know somewhat of what you'd like to see occur. This season will make it manifest even better than what you could've imagined.

If you've been wanting to meet your soulmate and have love in your life, Divine Timing Blessing Season One can deliver that miracle for you. And definitely meeting your twin flame or soulmate is a beautiful miracle; that occurrence can add immense joy to your life, so Jupiter is all about it.

I didn't get to tell you the rest of the story…when I moved away for graduate school with benevolent teacher planet of blessings, Jupiter in Aquarius, I not only had an Aquarius friend/boss (Anthony, who helped bridge the gap between where I was working and living to attend graduate school and receive my master's in holistic health), I also met my husband, who is also an Aquarius.

Of course, when I went off to graduate school, excited to pursue and explore knowledge of holistic health, mysticism, and spirituality, I also had a yearning to meet the man of my dreams. I knew from knowledge of my chart that it was going to happen, and I was so grateful miracles do exist. When you are in Divine Timing Blessings Season One, you have the golden ticket to accomplish anything – creating magnificence in your life you never deemed possible!

It's amazing to note that being a blessing to others offers an amount of benevolence to your own life. Let me explain…There's a saying that says to get what you want, you have to help others get what they want. When you become benevolent, offer good fortune, or are a blessing to others, I'm not speaking about working in a soup kitchen or volunteering, although you may do those things. It's about when you are good fortune to others, they happen to be a good fortune for you, just as the example I gave earlier when I was hired to work at that designer boutique while in graduate school and rented the loft. My new friend Anthony, who owned the loft and also owned the designer boutique I worked at in graduate school, his benevolence to me (hiring me and renting the loft to me) actually helped him out as I made him a lot of money.

What you are seeking is seeking you. You'll learn this experience while you're in Divine Timing Season One. Since you are in essence "Lady Luck," you bring luck to people which makes you highly desirable as a partner – in love, career, financial matters, marriage, and everything! This is your time, so seize the moment and make the most of this rare divine timing season as there will be a time when the divine timing season is over. This season repeats itself every 12 years, but you don't want to have to wait another 12 years for this season!

Nurture the Blessings
Divine Timing Blessing – Season One
Focus on the Blessings

1. You are gifted with the golden ticket.
2. Your benevolence and gift is that you are "lucky" for others, and people will feel and know this. This gives you access to VIPs and doors that were previously closed to you.
3. Take action; nothing happens by just thinking about it. You must take action.
4. During this miracle time, you may very well meet your soulmate.
5. Become Jupiter. Jupiter is the planet governing good fortune, luck, miracles, and benevolence. By becoming benevolent, you offer this gift to yourself.
6. Check out where your challenges are in the Navigate the Challenges sector. Be sure to starve that source of energy as much as possible and nurture your current blessing season. Starving does not mean avoidance. It means not to place all of your intention or power on your challenges. Give the intention and energy to your Nurture the Blessings season.
7. Focus on what you want to manifest in your life and what you want your reality to look like a year from now in life, career, and love. Make it happen!
8. Do a vision board.
9. Visualize your goals.
10. Be ready for your dreams and goals to happen.
11. Know what you desire in life; start to work toward it.
12. Dream big.

13. Follow your true, heartfelt passions.
14. Study, grow, travel.
15. See the magic in life, and manifest your best life.
16. Work toward what your vision of a beautiful life is.

<u>Nurture the Blessings</u>

Divine Timing Blessing – Season Two

You Are Highly Valued at This Time, Earning an Exceptional Income.

Divine Time You Are in Now

Pisces (February 19 - March 20)
You will experience Divine Timing Blessing Season Two during this time.

May 10, 2022, to October 28, 2022
December 20, 2022, to May 16, 2023
April 21, 2034, to April 29, 2035

Aries (March 21 - April 19)
You will experience Divine Timing Blessing Season Two during this time.

May 16, 2023, to May 25, 2024
April 29, 2035, to May 9, 2036
April 13, 2047, to April 22, 2048

Taurus (April 20 - May 20)
You will experience Divine Timing Blessing Season Two during this time.

May 25, 2024, to June 9, 2025
May 9, 2036, to May 23, 2037
April 22, 2048, to September 23, 2048
November 12, 2048, to May 5, 2049

Gemini (May 21 - June 20)
You will experience Divine Timing Blessing Season Two during this time.

June 9, 2025, to June 30, 2026
May 23, 2037, to June 12, 2038
September 23, 2048, to November 12, 2048
May 5, 2049, to September 27, 2049

Cancer (June 21 - July 22)
You will experience Divine Timing Blessing Season Two during this time.
June 30, 2026, to July 26, 2027
June 12, 2038, to November 16, 2038
January 16, 2039, to July 7, 2039

Leo (July 23 - August 22)
You will experience Divine Timing Blessing Season Two during this time.
July 26, 2027, to August 24, 2028
November 16, 2038, to January 16, 2039
July 7, 2039, to December 12, 2039
February 20, 2040, to August 5, 2040

Virgo (August 23 - September 22)
You will experience Divine Timing Blessing Season Two during this time.
August 24, 2028, to September 24, 2029
December 12, 2039, to February 20, 2040
August 5, 2040, to January 11, 2041
March 20, 2041, to September 5, 2041

Libra (September 23 - October 22)
You will experience Divine Timing Blessing Season Two during this time.
September 24, 2029, to October 22, 2030
January 11, 2041, to March 20, 2041
September 5, 2041, to February 8, 2042
April 24, 2042, to October 4, 2042

Scorpio (October 23 - November 21)
You will experience Divine Timing Blessing Season Two during this time.

October 22, 2030, to November 15, 2031

February 8, 2042, to April 24, 2042

October 4, 2043, to June 9, 2043

Sagittarius (November 22 - December 21)
You will experience Divine Timing Blessing Season Two during this time.

November 15, 2031, to April 11, 2032

June 26, 2032, to November 29, 2032

March 1, 2043, to June 9, 2043

October 26, 2043, to March 15, 2044

August 9, 2044, to November 4, 2044

Capricorn (December 22 - January 19)
You will experience Divine Timing Blessing Season Two during this time.

December 19, 2020, to May 13, 2021

July 28, 2021, to December 28, 2021

April 11, 2032, to June 26, 2032

November 29, 2032, to April 14, 2033

September 12, 2033, to December 1, 2033

March 15, 2044, to August 9, 2044

Aquarius (January 20 - February 18)
You will experience Divine Timing Blessing Season Two during this time.

May 13, 2021, to July 28, 2021

December 28, 2021, to May 10, 2022

October 28, 2022, to December 20, 2022

April 14, 2033, to September 12, 2033

December 1, 2033, to April 21, 2034

Nurture the Blessings
Divine Timing Blessing – Season Two

While you're experiencing Divine Timing Season Two, you're in for a time of earning a lot more money. Not only are you making more money and having a steady flow of income, you are also highly valued in your industry. Your earnings will be steady and plentiful, and if you work for an employer, it's a great time to ask for a raise. If you are in business for yourself, you should notice yourself signing on clients and projects that net you a healthy income. It's the work and earnings you gain from the work you do from day to day that is being blessed with good fortune.

As we look at Divine Timing Season Two, it's not only about the value we bring to our business or our employer. It's about what we value. During this time, you may note that you are being blessed with great income and also loving the means by which you are earning money. When you have this blessing season, you will not only make a great income but enjoy how you are earning it, as that is a part of this blessing season.

However, we should also note that you will be blessed not only with income but with what you value. It's been said time and time again, "Time is money, and money is time." This couldn't be truer, particularly in this Divine Time of Blessing Season Two. In this season, if time and spending treasured time with family is valuable to you, you may be granted the option to work remotely from home, be given a flexible schedule with unlimited vacation, or have more autonomy in your schedule. If you work for yourself and you've noticed that you haven't had the time with your spouse or family that you desire, you'll be able to create more balance somehow. The Universe will conspire to help you. Not only to have money as money is represented as energy on Earth and is energy, in essence, but the Universe will help you create that which you value.

If it's time, you'll have more time. If it's money, you'll have more money. And if it's both, you'll have both. You'll be able to blissfully earn a living, and the way you earn a living will be divinely protected. When you experience this beautiful blessing season, pay attention to the types of blessings that come your way as these can be cues to your best earning potential until your next Divine Timing Blessing Season Two, which will occur in 12 years. This season occurs every 12 years, all blessing seasons do, so it is imperative that we make the most of each and every one of them. Do not take your income or money for granted while your earnings are robust.

I suggest you do some investing for a rainy day, because the sun shines, and then sometime later, we experience rain. It's just part of the different seasons of life. If you've been hoping for a raise, that could really be a reality for you now. If you are happy at your job, then things will only get better! If you are unhappy at your job or in your business, Divine Blessing Season Two will provide ample opportunity for you to find a new job or the old one will simply get better. If you have a boss or employee who is making your life miserable, they may leave or be moved to a different department. This divine season will protect your interest in how you earn a living. If you are unhappy at work and earning a living isn't really a joy, then expect wonderful changes. Jupiter wants and believes that every experience should be one that brings you joy and happiness. This year will potentially bring you a new job and/or new earning opportunities you'll want to examine as the opportunities may pay more and better fit your life and situation at this time. Divine Timing Season Two will protect what you value. This year, your gift is in joyfully earning a living. If that is not your current situation or you feel ready for a change, this is a good year to make that change a reality and have the wind at your back and the road rising up to meet you. What a blessed year you have in store with this season that lasts roughly 12 months.

If you want to make the most of this season, I suggest you meditate on what you value and take action so this divine season can bring it to life for you!

Nurture the Blessings
Divine Timing Blessing – Season Two
Focus on the Blessings

What do I value, and how do I want to earn a living?

1. Getting a raise or earning more income
2. Earning a living joyfully
3. Work that brings you efficiency and joy
4. An improved work situation
5. Working on anything that will help you earn a better living
6. How you earn a living is protected.
7. Start a new job
8. Being of value and valued in your industry
9. If having trouble at work, it will get much better.
10. Earning a living will be a blessing as you focus on what you value.

<u>Nurture the Blessings</u>

Divine Timing Blessing – Season Three

You Are Blessed With the Key.

Divine Time You Are in Now

Aquarius (January 20 - February 18)
You will experience Divine Timing Blessing Season Three during this time.
May 10, 2022, to October 28, 2022
December 20, 2022, to May 16, 2023
April 21, 2034, to April 29, 2035

Pisces (February 19 - March 20)
You will experience Divine Timing Blessing Season Three during this time.
May 16, 2023, to May 25, 2024
April 29, 2035, to May 9, 2036
April 13, 2047, to April 22, 2048

Aries (March 21 - April 19)
You will experience Divine Timing Blessing Season Three during this time.
May 25, 2024, to June 9, 2025
May 9, 2036, to May 23, 2037
April 22, 2048, to September 23, 2048
November 12, 2048, to May 5, 2049

Taurus (April 20 - May 20)
You will experience Divine Timing Blessing Season Three during this time.
June 9, 2025, to June 30, 2026

May 23, 2037, to June 12, 2038
September 23, 2048, to November 12, 2048
May 5, 2049, to September 27, 2049

Gemini (May 21 - June 20)
You will experience Divine Timing Blessing Season Three during this time.
June 30, 2026, to July 26, 2027
June 12, 2038, to November 16, 2038
January 16, 2039, to July 7, 2039

Cancer (June 21 - July 22)
You will experience Divine Timing Blessing Season Three during this time.
July 26, 2027, to August 24, 2028
November 16, 2038, to January 16, 2039
July 7, 2039, to December 12, 2039
February 20, 2040, to August 5, 2040

Leo (July 23 - August 22)
You will experience Divine Timing Blessing Season Three during this time.
August 24, 2028, to September 24, 2029
December 12, 2039, to February 20, 2040
August 5, 2040, to January 11, 2041
March 20, 2041, to September 5, 2041

Virgo (August 23 - September 22)
You will experience Divine Timing Blessing Season Three during this time.
September 24, 2029, to October 22, 2030
January 11, 2041, to March 20, 2041
September 5, 2041, to February 8, 2042
April 24, 2042, to October 4, 2042

Libra (September 23 - October 22)
You will experience Divine Timing Blessing Season Three during this time.

October 22, 2030, to November 15, 2031

February 8, 2042, to April 24, 2042

October 4, 2043, to June 9, 2043

Scorpio (October 23 - November 21)
You will experience Divine Timing Blessing Season Three during this time.

November 15, 2031, to April 11, 2032

June 26, 2032, to November 29, 2032

March 1, 2043, to June 9, 2043

October 26, 2043, to March 15, 2044

August 9, 2044, to November 4, 2044

Sagittarius (November 22 - December 21)
You will experience Divine Timing Blessing Season Three during this time.

December 19, 2020, to May 13, 2021

July 28, 2021, to December 28, 2021

April 11, 2032, to June 26, 2032

November 29, 2032, to April 14, 2033

September 12, 2033, to December 1, 2033

March 15, 2044, to August 9, 2044

Capricorn (December 22 - January 19)
You will experience Divine Timing Blessing Season Three during this time.

May 13, 2021, to July 28, 2021

December 28, 2021, to May 10, 2022

October 28, 2022, to December 20, 2022

April 14, 2033, to September 12, 2033

December 1, 2033, to April 21, 2034

Nurture the Blessings
Divine Timing Blessing –
Season Three

When you're in Divine Timing Blessing Season Three, you have access to a diverse array of blessings that will add ease to your life in many ways! If communication is the key to success in all endeavors, then this year you shall have the key. Divine Timing Blessing Season Three emphasizes the importance of good communication. Excellent communication skills can get you into doors that are normally shut. Communication can heal a relationship that is hurting, and it can build a thriving and beneficial business partnership. It can create genius in many forms, such as music composition and any form of writing and public speaking.

When you get to experience Divine Timing Blessing Season Three, it introduces us to the concept of others. Blessing Season One focuses on who we are, Blessing Season Two on what we value, and Blessing Season Three welcomes communication, siblings, and even transportation. We'll get to that in a moment, if you've had your eye on that dazzling new car!

Let's talk about the topics of siblings, because while you're blessed to have the key of communication, you will also be a blessing to your siblings, and your siblings will be a blessing to you. This sector of life in Blessing Season Three offers protection to our siblings. It heals relationships if there have been any issues in the past and gives us an opportunity to come back together through communication. Even if your siblings are your best friends and you speak every day, your sibling will play a more prominent role in your life, and you're sure to have a lot of good moments together and be a beacon of light for one another.

My sisters and I are very close. My sisters are Love and Faith Hope (yes, our real names), and we do everything together. If you've read Blessing Season One when I spoke about this story, you'll relate here. When I took a journey to graduate school with one week's notice and was experiencing Blessing Season One, my sister Faith Hope was experiencing Blessing Season Three, blessings with communication, short-distance travel, and of course, siblings.

My sister magnetized a lot of the luck I experienced during my Divine Timing Blessing Season Three. I shared a story in Blessing Season One of some blessings that occurred for me during that season. If you did not read Blessing One yet, the complete reference is there. What I did not mention in Divine Timing Blessing Season One is when I was relocating with very little notice to go to graduate school and ended up working for Anthony (who is now my friend) who owned the building where I leased my loft and the designer fashion boutique in which he hired me in a moment of synchronicity, my sister Faith had mentioned to him at dinner that she thought it would be a great idea if I worked at the boutique while in grad school to make extra money to pay for the loft. My sister made the suggestion, and that led to my success and having an amazing time in grad school. My sister and I, along with our new friends, created life-long and outrageously fun memories. It was all part of a master plan that involved my sibling and communication!

Communication assures our success in many endeavors and relationships. This blessing season will now spoil you with the gift of gracious gab, writing, negotiations, contracts, sibling healing, blessings, and much more! Communication is such an essential skill for success in every area of life. Communication affects how well you are received. The gift of gab helps you make the sale, close the deal, have a good relationship with your romantic partner or spouse, or attract new love, if you are single. Communication is key, as they say, so this year, you shall have the key! Also, to note about siblings, if you have no siblings, please note that this blessing season also covers cousins as well. If you have been concerned for a sibling or siblings, Jupiter's healing energy will greatly assist with the healing of your sibling or sibling relationship. Yes, if your relationship with a sibling has been strained, you'll see miracles and improvements start very soon. Teacher Jupiter, which governs over the blessing seasons, can be likened to a fairy godmother who loves to show us that anything is possible, including healing, miracles, and communication that delivers you the key to happiness in every area of life.

Nurture the Blessings-Divine Timing Blessing – Season Three Focus on the Blessings

Your gifts in Divine Timing Blessing Season Three – siblings, communication, writing in all its forms, speaking, self-promotion, negotiation, and sales – will all shine bright for you.

1. Focus on negotiating excellent contracts and agreements.
2. Communicate! Take a public speaking class.
3. You will be a blessing to your siblings, and your siblings will be a blessing to you. Stay in contact with your sibling or siblings; you should see improvement with any difficulties, and blessings will flow between you.
4. Journal for healing – write, write, write your book, screenplay, or music, or take a workshop and/or class.
5. You have the key to communication! Use it wisely.
6. Enjoy short-distance travel to nearby towns for brief, nice vacations.
7. Upgrade your vehicle this year!
8. If single, ask your sibling for an introduction.
9. Utilize public relations and self-promotion.
10. Use your excellent communication skills to land big deals.

Nurture the Blessings

Divine Timing Blessing – Season Four

*Your Sense of Home, Family, and
Stability Are Being Blessed.*

Divine Time You Are in Now

Capricorn (December 22 - January 19)
You will experience Divine Timing Blessing Season Four during this time.

May 10, 2022, to October 28, 2022
December 20, 2022, to May 16, 2023
April 21, 2034, to April 29, 2035

Aquarius (January 20 - February 18)
You will experience Divine Timing Blessing Season Four during this time.

May 16, 2023, to May 25, 2024
April 29, 2035, to May 9, 2036
April 13, 2047, to April 22, 2048

Pisces (February 19 - March 20)
You will experience Divine Timing Blessing Season Four during this time.

May 25, 2024, to June 9, 2025
May 9, 2036, to May 23, 2037
April 22, 2048, to September 23, 2048
November 12, 2048, to May 5, 2049

Aries (March 21 - April 19)
You will experience Divine Timing Blessing Season Four during this time.

June 9, 2025, to June 30, 2026
May 23, 2037, to June 12, 2038
September 23, 2048, to November 12, 2048
May 5, 2049, to September 27, 2049

Taurus (April 20 - May 20)
You will experience Divine Timing Blessing Season Four during this time.
June 30, 2026, to July 26, 2027
June 12, 2038, to November 16, 2038
January 16, 2039, to July 7, 2039

Gemini (May 21 - June 20)
You will experience Divine Timing Blessing Season Four during this time.
July 26, 2027, to August 24, 2028
November 16, 2038, to January 16, 2039
July 7, 2039, to December 12, 2039
February 20, 2040, to August 5, 2040

Cancer (June 21 - July 22)
You will experience Divine Timing Blessing Season Four during this time.
August 24, 2028, to September 24, 2029
December 12, 2039, to February 20, 2040
August 5, 2040, to January 11, 2041
March 20, 2041, to September 5, 2041

Leo (July 23 - August 22)
You will experience Divine Timing Blessing Season Four during this time.
September 24, 2029, to October 22, 2030
January 11, 2041, to March 20, 2041
September 5, 2041, to February 8, 2042
April 24, 2042, to October 4, 2042

Virgo (August 23 - September 22)

You will experience Divine Timing Blessing Season Four during this time.

October 22, 2030, to November 15, 2031

February 8, 2042, to April 24, 2042

October 4, 2043, to June 9, 2043

Libra (September 23 - October 22)

You will experience Divine Timing Blessing Season Four during this time.

November 15, 2031, to April 11, 2032

June 26, 2032, to November 29, 2032

March 1, 2043, to June 9, 2043

October 26, 2043, to March 15, 2044

August 9, 2044, to November 4, 2044

Scorpio (October 23 - November 21)

You will experience Divine Timing Blessing Season Four during this time.

December 19, 2020, to May 13, 2021

July 28, 2021, to December 28, 2021

April 11, 2032, to June 26, 2032

November 29, 2032, to April 14, 2033

September 12, 2033, to December 1, 2033

March 15, 2044, to August 9, 2044

Sagittarius (November 22 - December 21)

You will experience Divine Timing Blessing Season Four during this time.

May 13, 2021, to July 28, 2021

December 28, 2021, to May 10, 2022

October 28, 2022, to December 20, 2022

April 14, 2033, to September 12, 2033

December 1, 2033, to April 21, 2034

Nurture the Blessings
Divine Timing Blessing –
Season Four

When you are experiencing Divine Timing Blessing Season Four, your life will have a feeling of stability. Divine Timing Blessing Season Four represents your physical home, family, parents, and real estate. There is so much about this divine timing blessing season that you'll love.

This is a time in which your family, parents, and home are places of central joy and empowerment. If you've been looking for new real estate, you'll find something very special at this time and win the bid. It could be for investment, or it could be your new family home. It's a wonderful time to build a new home or do renovations on your current home. You will love whatever renovations you do during this season, and your family will enjoy these improvements for many years to come.

If you're looking to lease a new condo, townhouse, or apartment, you will find a space full of light and beyond what you would have thought you could find. You'll welcome into your life that which you desire to achieve an overall sense of stability. If you are wanting love in your life, your parents might just play matchmaker and make the introduction.

If you're in a relationship with someone, this is potentially the season when you would move in together. This season is really about what you need to feel stable, happy, and joyful at home. Whether that's a new design on your current home, a new home, or a partner to share your home with, this season will help you achieve stability. Also, Divine Timing Blessing Season Four serves as extra protection for your home, family, and parents.

If you've been concerned about your parents' well-being, Divine Timing Blessing Season Four is a time when you can see wonderful progress with your parents' well-being, and you will play a part in that. Your family and parents will also be lucky for you. If you need help with anything that your family or parents can provide, you will get the help you need.

It's a time of great blessings that can deliver so much to your life if you focus on nurturing this blessing season – as opposed to your challenges.

Divine Timing Blessing Season Four is also divine protection for your parents and shows that your parents and/or family will be a blessing to you. If your parents have passed, this divine season will still be a blessing to you in so many ways. If you have been concerned about a family member or parent, Jupiter will be such a healing force here. Have you wanted to invest in a new home or investment property? That area of life will be so very gifted for you!

Your home life should start to feel more stable too, as blessings will come to your family and through your family. With this season, stability and family will be hallmarks of happiness and joy for you. Being at home will offer such great peace and delight, and home life will be the best life! If you're in real estate or design or have a career related to property, this transit will also fuel your career. Regardless of what you do for a living, Divine Timing Season Four is such a welcome season as it is known as the anchor of stability. If things are good at home, things are so much sweeter everywhere!

This is the best season in the last 12 years to focus on finding the right home or doing renovation on a home or property you already own. Family, whatever you deem that to be, will be beyond blessed in structure. During this season, family and home will be such a source of love and blessings for you!

Nurture the Blessings
Divine Timing Blessing –
Season Four
Focus on the Blessings

Nurture and focus on family structure and home as your source of blessings.

1. Make home a beacon of wellness.
2. Spend time with family at home.
3. Have children spend time with your parents.
4. Start work on a dream renovation project.
5. Have parents or grandparents pray for your children.
6. Move in with a love, if you're ready.
7. Buy a house or other property.
8. Nurture time with family.
9. Spend time at home.
10. Hire cleaning staff, if needed, and make your home your haven of peace.

Nurture the Blessings

Divine Timing Blessing – Season Five

You Are Being Blessed With Creativity, Romance, Love, and Children.

Divine Time You Are in Now

Sagittarius (November 22 - December 21)
You will experience Divine Timing Blessing Season Five during this time.

May 10, 2022, to October 28, 2022

December 20, 2022, to May 16, 2023

April 21, 2034, to April 29, 2035

Capricorn (December 22 - January 19)
You will experience Divine Timing Blessing Season Five during this time.

May 16, 2023, to May 25, 2024

April 29, 2035, to May 9, 2036

April 13, 2047, to April 22, 2048

Aquarius (January 20 - February 18)
You will experience Divine Timing Blessing Season Five during this time.

May 25, 2024, to June 9, 2025

May 9, 2036, to May 23, 2037

April 22, 2048, to September 23, 2048

November 12, 2048, to May 5, 2049

Pisces (February 19 - March 20)
You will experience Divine Timing Blessing Season Five during this time.

June 9, 2025, to June 30, 2026
May 23, 2037, to June 12, 2038
September 23, 2048, to November 12, 2048
May 5, 2049, to September 27, 2049

Aries (March 21 - April 19)
You will experience Divine Timing Blessing Season Five during this time.
June 30, 2026, to July 26, 2027
June 12, 2038, to November 16, 2038
January 16, 2039, to July 7, 2039

Taurus (April 20 - May 20)
You will experience Divine Timing Blessing Season Five during this time.
July 26, 2027, to August 24, 2028
November 16, 2038, to January 16, 2039
July 7, 2039, to December 12, 2039
February 20, 2040, to August 5, 2040

Gemini (May 21 - June 20)
You will experience Divine Timing Blessing Season Five during this time.
August 24, 2028, to September 24, 2029
December 12, 2039, to February 20, 2040
August 5, 2040, to January 11, 2041
March 20, 2041, to September 5, 2041

Cancer (June 21 - July 22)
You will experience Divine Timing Blessing Season Five during this time.
September 24, 2029, to October 22, 2030
January 11, 2041, to March 20, 2041
September 5, 2041, to February 8, 2042
April 24, 2042, to October 4, 2042

Leo (July 23 - August 22)
You will experience Divine Timing Blessing Season Five during this time.

October 22, 2030, to November 15, 2031

February 8, 2042, to April 24, 2042

October 4, 2045, to June 9, 2043

Virgo (August 23 - September 22)
You will experience Divine Timing Blessing Season Five during this time.

November 15, 2031, to April 11, 2032

June 26, 2032, to November 29, 2032

March 1, 2043, to June 9, 2043

October 26, 2043, to March 15, 2044

August 9, 2044, to November 4, 2044

Libra (September 23 - October 22)
You will experience Divine Timing Blessing Season Five during this time.

December 19, 2020, to May 13, 2021

July 28, 2021, to December 28, 2021

April 11, 2032, to June 26, 2032

November 29, 2032, to April 14, 2033

September 12, 2033, to December 1, 2033

March 15, 2044, to August 9, 2044

Scorpio (October 23 - November 21)
You will experience Divine Timing Blessing Season Five during this time.

May 13, 2021, to July 28, 2021

December 28, 2021, to May 10, 2022

October 28, 2022, to December 20, 2022

April 14, 2033, to September 12, 2033

December 1, 2033, to April 21, 2034

Nurture the Blessings
Divine Timing Blessing – Season Five

When you enter into the season of Divine Timing Blessing Season Five, you're in for many blessings and surprises! This divine blessing season can deliver so much good news to your life in a short span of time.

If you would like more love and romance in your life, this divine timing blessing season can deliver just that. This season can help you establish more love, fun, and romance in a current relationship or bring new love and romance into your life.

If you would like to adopt or conceive children, this is the year you could find out you're expecting. If you've been having trouble conceiving, this blessing season can help you conceive.

This divine blessing season is also about having recreation and fun in your life and the ability to let loose and enjoy life. If you work in a creative field, you will be extra creative and have extra luck. Divine Timing Blessing Season Five encourages having a childlike sense of play and a childlike sense of wonder. This is why creative problem solvers are able to come up with genius solutions with ease as part of creativity is being able to see wonder and magic in everything and that the impossible is possible.

This divine season should add a sense of fun to your everyday life. What a fabulous season you have before you! If you have been searching for true love and romance in your life or just want to have more fun, romance, and love with your current partner, you are very fortunate because this blessing season will gift you this. If you have been trying to conceive or adopt, this season of blessings and benevolence can deliver happy news from the stork! This year, if you have children, from toddlers to adults, your offspring will be divinely protected.

This divine blessing season will also offer you blessings and protection for your children, and your children will offer you much joy and happiness. Life, love, and the pursuit of happiness are about to get more fun!

You'll be able to relax and have more fun than you've had in a long time. Life will be easier and flow better. If you are in a creative field or enjoy any of the creative arts, such as creative writing, theater, and visual arts, you will find lots of opportunities to create this year. Embracing your creative side will not only brighten your life path at this time, it could be lucrative as well.

However, if you create just for the love of it, you'll benefit in emotional, mental, and spiritual wellness. If you are in a creative field professionally or were in a creative field but gave that up for a "real job," now may be the time to embrace the arts again. Life is about to be fun again!

Nurture the Blessings
Divine Timing Blessing – Season Five
Focus on the Blessings

I create a life full of love, creativity, fun, romance, and magic.

1. Invite more love and romance in your life.
2. If married, have more fun together and more dates, day or night.
3. If single, meet a new love.
4. Work in the arts.
5. Create, create, create.
6. Have a baby.
7. Lighten up; be childlike in your approach to life.
8. Adopt.
9. Foster a child or children in need.
10. Your children, if you have them, will be blessed and excel and bring joy to your life.

Nurture the Blessings

Divine Timing Blessing – Season Six

Your Vitality, Health, and Work Are Receiving Miracle Blessings Now.

Divine Time You Are in Now

Scorpio (October 23 - November 21)
You will experience Divine Timing Blessing Season Six during this time.

May 10, 2022, to October 28, 2022

December 20, 2022, to May 16, 2023

April 21, 2034, to April 29, 2035

Sagittarius (November 22 - December 21)
You will experience Divine Timing Blessing Season Six during this time.

May 16, 2023, to May 25, 2024

April 29, 2035, to May 9, 2036

April 13, 2047, to April 22, 2048

Capricorn (December 22 - January 19)
You will experience Divine Timing Blessing Season Six during this time.

May 25, 2024, to June 9, 2025

May 9, 2036, to May 23, 2037

April 22, 2048, to September 23, 2048

November 12, 2048, to May 5, 2049

Aquarius (January 20 - February 18)
You will experience Divine Timing Blessing Season Six during this time.

June 9, 2025, to June 30, 2026
May 23, 2037, to June 12, 2038
September 23, 2048, to November 12, 2048
May 5, 2049, to September 27, 2049

Pisces (February 19 - March 20)
You will experience Divine Timing Blessing Season Six during this time.
June 30, 2026, to July 26, 2027
June 12, 2038, to November 16, 2038
January 16, 2039, to July 7, 2039

Aries (March 21 - April 19)
You will experience Divine Timing Blessing Season Six during this time.
July 26, 2027, to August 24, 2028
November 16, 2038, to January 16, 2039
July 7, 2039, to December 12, 2039
February 20, 2040, to August 5, 2040

Taurus (April 20 - May 20)
You will experience Divine Timing Blessing Season Six during this time.
August 24, 2028, to September 24, 2029
December 12, 2039, to February 20, 2040
August 5, 2040, to January 11, 2041
March 20, 2041, to September 5, 2041

Gemini (May 21 - June 20)
You will experience Divine Timing Blessing Season Six during this time.
September 24, 2029, to October 22, 2030
January 11, 2041, to March 20, 2041
September 5, 2041, to February 8, 2042
April 24, 2042, to October 4, 2042

Cancer (June 21 - July 22)

You will experience Divine Timing Blessing Season Six during this time.

October 22, 2030, to November 15, 2031

February 8, 2042, to April 24, 2042

October 4, 2043, to June 9, 2043

Leo (July 23 - August 22)

You will experience Divine Timing Blessing Season Six during this time.

November 15, 2031, to April 11, 2032

June 26, 2032, to November 29, 2032

March 1, 2043, to June 9, 2043

October 26, 2043, to March 15, 2044

August 9, 2044, to November 4, 2044

Virgo (August 23 - September 22)

You will experience Divine Timing Blessing Season Six during this time.

December 19, 2020, to May 13, 2021

July 28, 2021, to December 28, 2021

April 11, 2032, to June 26, 2032

November 29, 2032, to April 14, 2033

September 12, 2033, to December 1, 2033

March 15, 2044, to August 9, 2044

Libra (September 23 - October 22)

You will experience Divine Timing Blessing Season Six during this time.

May 13, 2021, to July 28, 2021

December 28, 2021, to May 10, 2022

October 28, 2022, to December 20, 2022

April 14, 2033, to September 12, 2033

December 1, 2033, to April 21, 2034

Nurture the Blessings
Divine Timing Blessing – Season Six

During Divine Timing Blessing Season Six, you can achieve so much and add wonderful productivity to your life. This is a divine season where work is play and play is work. This is due to the fact that this season impacts your daily routines and how you get things done. You'll find the wind at your back and the roads rising up to meet you as you go throughout your day. If you wanted to find a fitness routine and stick to it, this is the time you would find one that works for you. If you desire to go on a new nutrition program and adjust your daily eating habits, this is the time when you can get in shape and make lifestyle changes that will impact your health and well-being for good. Divine Timing Season Six also impacts your physical health. If you've gone through any time of stress or illness in the body, this will be a healing time for you, and it could very well bring miracles to your health and well-being.

Your daily goals will happen with ease. Tackling your to-do list will be no problem. This divine season blesses you with vitality in your physical body, daily routines, work, fitness, and physical well-being. During this time, your daily work will actually bring you joy. Your talent and skills will be in high demand, and you will be appreciated at your place of work which includes a business you own and the clients you work with or an actual employer. Either way, you'll be appreciated and respected at work.

If you have been unhappy at work, work will start to be a place of joy and happiness. Miraculous changes will be made to your benefit. Higher ups and direct reports will either be supportive of you or leave or change departments, and you'll get a better supervisor or direct report. Perhaps, you will move jobs altogether. If you are your own boss, you'll also enjoy the work you do and have favor in your marketplace.

Divine Timing Blessing Season Six wants to help you in your daily life and routines, and work is where we spend a huge percentage of our life, time, and energy. It's hard to be happy if work makes you miserable. In your work life and daily routines, life will start to just flow! You may take a new job during this season, or the old one will get much better. Even if you are deeply satisfied with your employment, life at work during this season will get even better and flow with ease.

Divine Timing Blessing Season Six is not all about work and six-pack abs. This divine season can also help your love life. The first obvious way is when we feel good about ourselves and are healthy, fit, and feeling vibrant, we are more confident, and confidence is definitely attractive. I'm not saying you have to be in tip-top shape to attract love; everyone's body type is different. However, feeling healthy and vibrant can only increase your feelings of confidence in attracting love.

The second way Divine Timing Blessing Season Six can help your love life is by meeting someone in one of the blessing areas. That would be in a fitness class, yoga, or your favorite gym. Also, if single and wanting a romantic relationship, you may meet someone single through work who is also wanting a relationship. If you are in a relationship or married, you can add fun and joy to your relationship by simply working out together, taking walks, or working out with a personal trainer. You choose the activity – just get started. It will create more happiness and romance in your relationship, and you can get healthier and fit together. So many gifts can happen for you in this divine season of blessing.

As mentioned before, this divine blessing season also rules health and fitness, and if you've been procrastinating getting healthy, this is the time to make it happen! This is the best time in the last 12 years to start a new fitness routine or change eating habits, leading to better health. This divine blessing season will help you make healthier choices, leading to your success. While working on self-care in this divine blessing season of fitness, wellness routines will be helpful for you in navigating any challenges this year. You'll find spending time with a wellness and fitness routine that makes you feel vibrant is a welcome blessing.

Nurture the Blessings
Divine Timing Blessing – Season Six
Focus on the Blessings

Focus on creating a daily, work, wellness, and fitness routine you love.

1. Focus on loving your day-to-day work.
2. Start a new fitness routine.
3. Single love may bloom at the gym or work.
4. Couples add bliss to your relationship – enjoy fitness together.
5. Focus on self-care.
6. Work with a nutritionist or coach; find the right meal plan.
7. Apply for a new job.
8. Create an amazing work environment.
9. Pursue greatness at work. Whether you work for a company or for your own business. Work is work.
10. Create a daily routine you love.

<u>Nurture the Blessings</u>

Divine Timing Blessing – Season Seven

You Are Blessed in Partnership and Marriage.

Divine Time You Are in Now

Libra (September 23 - October 22)
You will experience Divine Timing Blessing Season Seven during this time.
May 10, 2022, to October 28, 2022
December 20, 2022, to May 16, 2023
April 21, 2034, to April 29, 2035

Scorpio (October 23 - November 21)
You will experience Divine Timing Blessing Season Seven during this time.
May 16, 2023, to May 25, 2024
April 29, 2035, to May 9, 2036
April 13, 2047, to April 22, 2048

Sagittarius (November 22 - December 21)
You will experience Divine Timing Blessing Season Seven during this time.
May 25, 2024, to June 9, 2025
May 9, 2036, to May 23, 2037
April 22, 2048, to September 23, 2048
 November 12, 2048, to May 5, 2049

Capricorn (December 22 - January 19)
You will experience Divine Timing Blessing Season Seven during this time.
June 9, 2025, to June 30, 2026

May 23, 2037, to June 12, 2038
September 23, 2048, to November 12, 2048
May 5, 2049, to September 27, 2049

Aquarius (January 20 - February 18)
You will experience Divine Timing Blessing Season Seven during this time.
June 30, 2026, to July 26, 2027
June 12, 2038, to November 16, 2038
January 16, 2039, to July 7, 2039

Pisces (February 19 - March 20)
You will experience Divine Timing Blessing Season Seven during this time.
July 26, 2027, to August 24, 2028
November 16, 2038, to January 16, 2039
July 7, 2039, to December 12, 2039
February 20, 2040, to August 5, 2040

Aries (March 21 - April 19)
You will experience Divine Timing Blessing Season Seven during this time.
August 24, 2028, to September 24, 2029
December 12, 2039, to February 20, 2040
August 5, 2040, to January 11, 2041
March 20, 2041, to September 5, 2041

Taurus (April 20 - May 20)
You will experience Divine Timing Blessing Season Seven during this time.
September 24, 2029, to October 22, 2030
January 11, 2041, to March 20, 2041
September 5, 2041, to February 8, 2042
April 24, 2042, to October 4, 2042

Gemini (May 21 - June 20)

You will experience Divine Timing Blessing Season Seven during this time.

October 22, 2030, to November 15, 2031

February 8, 2042, to April 24, 2042

October 4, 2043, to June 9, 2043

Cancer (June 21 - July 22)

You will experience Divine Timing Blessing Season Seven during this time.

November 15, 2031, to April 11, 2032

June 26, 2032, to November 29, 2032

March 1, 2043, to June 9, 2043

October 26, 2043, to March 15, 2044

August 9, 2044, to November 4, 2044

Leo (July 23 - August 22)

You will experience Divine Timing Blessing Season Seven during this time.

December 19, 2020, to May 13, 2021

July 28, 2021, to December 28, 2021

April 11, 2032, to June 26, 2032

November 29, 2032, to April 14, 2033

September 12, 2033, to December 1, 2033

March 15, 2044, to August 9, 2044

Virgo (August 23 - September 22)

You will experience Divine Timing Blessing Season Seven during this time.

May 13, 2021, to July 28, 2021

December 28, 2021, to May 10, 2022

October 28, 2022, to December 20, 2022

April 14, 2033, to September 12, 2033

December 1, 2033, to April 21, 2034

Nurture the Blessings
Divine Timing Blessing – Season Seven

When you're in Divine Timing Blessing Season Seven, you are in one of the most benevolent blessing seasons that you will encounter. This divine blessing season is one of my all-time favorites. This season gives you wonderful favor to attract amazing partnerships in business, love, and marriage. This is the best time in over 12 years to meet and marry your soulmate.

The only other time that is perhaps as good as this time for potentially meeting your soulmate is Divine Timing Blessing Season One when you become a source of benevolence and blessings for others. However, Divine Timing Blessing Season Seven goes a step further and everyone wants to partner with you. During this divine time, you may very well get engaged or married or simply meet the one.

The types of romantic interest you attract during this season will be more serious and commitment minded then in seasons past. This is a very different season than Divine Timing Blessing Season Five. Divine Timing Blessing Season Five gives you the lightness, playfulness, fun, and romance of dating. While Season Seven gives you a commitment-minded partner – a partner who wants a long-term relationship that may very well lead to engagement and marriage. Season Five can deliver love and marriage as well, yet in season five, it may take two years of dating, to get to engagement — depending on your chart.

Going into this divine timing season, you may already be in a serious relationship, and if things are going well, you will more than likely take the next step of commitment. If you are married, Divine

Blessing Season Seven will help you and your spouse to thrive, now more than ever.

If the waters of your marriage have been turbulent, Divine Timing Season Seven can bring healing through work with a therapist or coach. This season can indeed bring miracles in this area. If things have been troubled for some time, and there is no pathway forward. For example, if you're in an unfaithful or abusive marriage or relationship, this divine season will give you the courage to leave.

The Universe wants to bless you to be in a good union that is healthy, happy, and for your highest good. All partnerships and marriages will have their difficult moments – that is just part of being two different, independent people, two people with different minds, thought processes, strengths, and weaknesses. Yet in situations like abuse, etc., the only path forward may be the blessing of freeing yourself from the marriage. In that case, the Universe will see to it that you are blessed with the courage to create a more solid partnership in the future. During Divine Timing Blessing Season Seven, you will also create excellent business partnerships that will help you be more successful. This divine timing blessing season also gives you favor in any court proceedings. You will have the right attorneys and the favor of the judge. Blessing Season Seven is like having the golden ticket in regard to any and all forms of partnerships. This is such a dynamic time!

Nurture the Blessings Divine Timing Blessing – Season Seven Focus on the Blessings

Nurture and focus should be on forming effective and powerful partnerships.

1. Marriage
2. Business partnerships
3. Attorneys and other partnerships
4. If single, work with a matchmaker to find "the one."
5. If married or living together, this season will be a further blessing for your relationship. You and your partner will thrive.
6. Do a vision board as to what you would like to manifest with this rare and beautiful divine blessing season.
7. It's a great time to start a business with a partner.
8. Get engaged.
9. Meet serious partners who want marriage.
10. Heal your marriage with counseling or coaching or gain the courage to leave, if in an abusive relationship or with an unfaithful partner.

<u>Nurture the Blessings</u>

Divine Timing Blessing – Season Eight

I Am Blessed to Finance My Dreams and Goals.

Divine Time You Are in Now

Virgo (August 23 - September 22)
You will experience Divine Timing Blessing Season Eight during this time.
May 10, 2022, to October 28, 2022
December 20, 2022, to May 16, 2023
April 21, 2034, to April 29, 2035

Libra (September 23 - October 22)
You will experience Divine Timing Blessing Season Eight during this time.
May 16, 2023, to May 25, 2024
April 29, 2035, to May 9, 2036
April 13, 2047, to April 22, 2048

Scorpio (October 23 - November 21)
You will experience Divine Timing Blessing Season Eight during this time.
May 25, 2024, to June 9, 2025
May 9, 2036, to May 23, 2037
April 22, 2048, to September 23, 2048
November 12, 2048, to May 5, 2049

Sagittarius (November 22 - December 21)
You will experience Divine Timing Blessing Season Eight during this time.
June 9, 2025, to June 30, 2026

May 23, 2037, to June 12, 2038
September 23, 2048, to November 12, 2048
May 5, 2049, to September 27, 2049

Capricorn (December 22 - January 19)
You will experience Divine Timing Blessing Season Eight during this time.
June 30, 2026, to July 26, 2027
June 12, 2038, to November 16, 2038
January 16, 2039, to July 7, 2039

Aquarius (January 20 - February 18)
You will experience Divine Timing Blessing Season Eight during this time.
July 26, 2027, to August 24, 2028
November 16, 2038, to January 16, 2039
July 7, 2039, to December 12, 2039
February 20, 2040, to August 5, 2040

Pisces (February 19 - March 20)
You will experience Divine Timing Blessing Season Eight during this time.
August 24, 2028, to September 24, 2029
December 12, 2039, to February 20, 2040
August 5, 2040, to January 11, 2041
March 20, 2041, to September 5, 2041

Aries (March 21 - April 19)
You will experience Divine Timing Blessing Season Eight during this time.
September 24, 2029, to October 22, 2030
January 11, 2041, to March 20, 2041
September 5, 2041, to February 8, 2042
April 24, 2042, to October 4, 2042

Taurus (April 20 - May 20)
You will experience Divine Timing Blessing Season Eight during this time.

October 22, 2030, to November 15, 2031
February 8, 2042, to April 24, 2042
October 4, 2043, to June 9, 2043

Gemini (May 21 - June 20)
You will experience Divine Timing Blessing Season Eight during this time.

November 15, 2031, to April 11, 2032
June 26, 2032, to November 29, 2032
March 1, 2043, to June 9, 2043
October 26, 2043, to March 15, 2044
August 9, 2044, to November 4, 2044

Cancer (June 21 - July 22)
You will experience Divine Timing Blessing Season Eight during this time.

December 19, 2020, to May 13, 2021
July 28, 2021, to December 28, 2021
April 11, 2032, to June 26, 2032
November 29, 2032, to April 14, 2033
September 12, 2033, to December 1, 2033
March 15, 2044, to August 9, 2044

Leo (July 23 - August 22)
You will experience Divine Timing Blessing Season Eight during this time.

May 13, 2021, to July 28, 2021
December 28, 2021, to May 10, 2022
October 28, 2022, to December 20, 2022
April 14, 2033, to September 12, 2033
December 1, 2033, to April 21, 2034

Nurture the Blessings
Divine Timing Blessing – Season Eight

When entering into Divine Timing Blessing Season Eight, your financial net worth can improve greatly! This is a great time to learn about financial strategy and investing and to finance big dreams and goals! Divine Timing Blessing Season Eight can deliver you a new mortgage loan for a property, a business loan or grant, an investor for your business, a big sale or deal, an inheritance, and manifestation of any dream that requires financial backing.

Your blessings will be in the form of "money, money, money, money ... money," as the song by the O'Jays states. With Divine Timing Blessing Season Eight, you can expect lots of financial opportunities coming into your life through various sources, setting up a divine blessing season for great financial success. Am I speaking your language? Yep, I thought so! With Divine Blessing Season Eight, you will be blessed in financing big dreams. This divine season of blessing governs over mortgages, sales, residual sales, loans, the stock market, venture capital, inheritances, taxes, loans, and debt.

If you've been hoping to get out of debt and pay off your creditors, this is the year to make a simple plan to make great strides in setting up your financial future. If you desire to get a loan or mortgage, you can see that happen this year, if you take action!

Would you like to start a career in finance, trading, or the stock market? This would be the year to do that. If there is sincere interest, go for it!

If you've been awaiting a settlement payment from an insurance payout or, say, an inheritance or split of assets, you'll be highly favored to see that settlement soon. This is the year to open a savings account or a mutual fund for financial success. There are so many potential manifestations of how this blessing season might take shape for you.

If you are in sales or are an entrepreneur, excellent! You can and should see huge gains this year. This is the financial house in which you finance big dreams. I'm so thrilled for you. It's time to make your financial dreams a reality.

This is a year that your finances will get a huge boost. Divine Blessing Season Eight is blessing you with funding for big dreams! If you've wanted to get on the hit show *Shark Tank*, for example, this is the year to get your dream funded. This is due to your current blessing season, Divine Timing Blessing Season Eight. This season governs investments, sales, mortgages, and venture capital—in essence, other people's money.

Divine Blessing Season Two is your other financial season and rules money you earn. This is different; Divine Timing Blessing Season Eight represents money, taxes, investments, venture capital, sales, and these areas of life. For example, if you're trying to refinance a mortgage or get a new mortgage approval, you will get help from the Universe. If you're in sales, the stock market, and/or looking for venture capital, or would like to get your taxes reassessed and lowered, that will flow easily for you now. If you are in sales, you will notice you are one of the top salespeople in your organization or firm.

If you manage a sales team or have your own business, your sales team will do exceptionally well now, and sales will be robust. Your organization will greatly benefit as will all of the people under your direction. This is your time.

For now, it's a great time to make financial deals, pull in venture capitalists and investors, and refinance. In order to nurture this part of life, it is imperative that you start work now. If you are hoping to refinance or purchase a home with a new mortgage and need to work on any credit discrepancies, those can easily be resolved now. If you would like to improve your credit score, you can easily get your credit score to soar by making arrangements to pay off bills and get a paid-in-full settlement report on your credit, if your credit was potentially hurt through debt or divorce, for instance. You can negotiate easily with creditors now and get these issues and other financial situations worked out greatly in your favor. Any business debts can easily be resolved at this point.

At the end of this transit, you should be able to create a completely new and improved financial situation – one that you love! This will take focus, nurturing the correct source ... that would be this area of life, the area of life the Universe is assisting you with! Also, it is important to note that Divine Blessing Season Eight not only governs finance, such as venture capital, creditors, and sales, but also prize winnings, such as lottery wins. Do try your hand at a few lotto tickets this year and other prize drawings. However, success here is rarer, and the odds are slim when trying to win the lottery. But if not you, then who? So, go ahead and play.

Lastly, Divine Timing Blessing Season Eight, which is blessing your life right now, governs over surgery. If you are in need of a surgical procedure, do it now. You are supremely blessed for excellent results. This is your time to create the success you've always desired in your finances.

"Anyone can become a millionaire, but to become a billionaire you need an astrologer."
— JP Morgan,
Founder of Chase Bank

Nurture the Blessings Divine Timing Blessing – Season Eight Focus on the Blessings

Focus on getting finances in a powerful place!

1. Work diligently to start a new savings plan.
2. Pay off debt to improve credit score.
3. Invest in the stock market or mutual funds.
4. Get a settlement completed.
5. Surgery could be helpful, if needed.
6. Apply for a mortgage.
7. Look toward sales and residuals.
8. Finance a business with venture capital.
9. Get an angel investor for a business idea.
10. Set up a retirement plan for a prosperous future.

<u>Nurture the Blessings</u>

Divine Timing Blessing – Season Nine

The World Is Your Oyster –
You Are Blessed in Higher Education,
International Travel, and More!

Divine Time You Are in Now

Leo (July 23 - August 22)
You will experience Divine Timing Blessing Season Nine during this time.

May 10, 2022, to October 28, 2022

December 20, 2022, to May 16, 2023

April 21, 2034, to April 29, 2035

Virgo (August 23 - September 22)
You will experience Divine Timing Blessing Season Nine during this time.

May 16, 2023, to May 25, 2024

April 29, 2035, to May 9, 2036

April 13, 2047, to April 22, 2048

Libra (September 23 - October 22)
You will experience Divine Timing Blessing Season Nine during this time.

May 25, 2024, to June 9, 2025

May 9, 2036, to May 23, 2037

April 22, 2048, to September 23, 2048

November 12, 2048, to May 5, 2049

Scorpio (October 23 - November 21)
You will experience Divine Timing Blessing Season Nine during this time.

June 9, 2025, to June 30, 2026

May 23, 2037, to June 12, 2038

September 23, 2048, to November 12, 2048

May 5, 2049, to September 27, 2049

Sagittarius (November 22 - December 21)
You will experience Divine Timing Blessing Season Nine during this time.

June 30, 2026, to July 26, 2027

June 12, 2038, to November 16, 2038

January 16, 2039, to July 7, 2039

Capricorn (December 22 - January 19)
You will experience Divine Timing Blessing Season Nine during this time.

July 26, 2027, to August 24, 2028

November 16, 2038, to January 16, 2039

July 7, 2039, to December 12, 2039

February 20, 2040, to August 5, 2040

Aquarius (January 20 - February 18)
You will experience Divine Timing Blessing Season Nine during this time.

August 24, 2028, to September 24, 2029

December 12, 2039, to February 20, 2040

August 5, 2040, to January 11, 2041

March 20, 2041, to September 5, 2041

Pisces (February 19 - March 20)
You will experience Divine Timing Blessing Season Nine during this time.

September 24, 2029, to October 22, 2030

January 11, 2041, to March 20, 2041

September 5, 2041, to February 8, 2042

April 24, 2042, to October 4, 2042

Aries (March 21 - April 19)
You will experience Divine Timing Blessing Season Nine during this time.

October 22, 2030, to November 15, 2031

February 8, 2042, to April 24, 2042

October 4, 2043, to June 9, 2043

Taurus (April 20 - May 20)
You will experience Divine Timing Blessing Season Nine during this time.

November 15, 2031, to April 11, 2032

June 26, 2032, to November 29, 2032

March 1, 2043, to June 9, 2043

October 26, 2043, to March 15, 2044

August 9, 2044, to November 4, 2044

Gemini (May 21 - June 20)
You will experience Divine Timing Blessing Season Nine during this time.

December 19, 2020, to May 13, 2021

July 28, 2021, to December 28, 2021

April 11, 2032, to June 26, 2032

November 29, 2032, to April 14, 2033

September 12, 2033, to December 1, 2033

March 15, 2044, to August 9, 2044

Cancer (June 21 - July 22)
You will experience Divine Timing Blessing Season Nine during this time.

May 13, 2021, to July 28, 2021

December 28, 2021, to May 10, 2022
October 28, 2022, to December 20, 2022
April 14, 2033, to September 12, 2033
December 1, 2033, to April 21, 2034

Nurture the Blessings
Divine Timing Blessing –
Season Nine

When you are entering into Divine Timing Blessing Season Nine, get ready to expand your ideas and experiences and increase what you know about the world at large. Divine Timing Season Nine gifts you with opportunities to travel abroad, learn a foreign language, and express your ideas to the world.

Divine Timing Blessing Season Nine governs over the sharing of ideas through publishing, television broadcasting, publicity, and public relations. Divine Timing Blessing Season Nine can bring you so many opportunities that will make your life exciting!

There are so many ways to use the good coming into your life!

Life is about to get really exciting! This Divine Timing Blessing Season Nine is all about expanding your mind through exploration and adventure. You'll go back to school to get an MBA, master's, PhD, or other advanced degree with which you will thrive. Also, foreign and international people, places, and relations will be highly favored. Perhaps, you and your family will welcome a foreign-exchange student into your home, or you might decide to relocate overseas to another country of interest; that is a divine way to use this energy. Wonderful experiences await you on your adventure.

If you are in publishing or broadcasting, what a fabulous time it is to get your book or article published or to get your television series going. You can also start by writing a blog or starting your own successful YouTube station, all very much blessed by this transit. If you're an actor, television will be the way to go over film, as film is governed by Divine Timing Blessing Season Twelve. This is the time to think big, dream big, and chart your path of discovery and knowledge. Teacher Jupiter, offering its benevolence to your Divine

Timing Blessing Season Nine, will bode well for you in this season of exploration! This divine season will offer you support in many other areas of life as well, but your most focused efforts should be concentrated on the aforementioned activities. Life's blessings will begin to shine in so many areas, so get ready to pack a bag and learn and grow! Do you want to travel to distant lands? You will have ample opportunities this year. Would you like to study abroad? You could not have picked a better time. Blessings and opportunities will be plentiful in this sector of life, coming in the way of a plethora of educational opportunities.

Religion and philosophy are also covered by Divine Timing Blessing Season Nine as opposed to spirituality which occurs in Divine Timing Blessing Season Twelve. Are you hoping to find a good church in which you can feel a sense of community, or are you studying theology? Goals in this area will go smoothly, and you'll have the drive to go forth and make it happen. If you are going back to school to finish up an undergraduate or advanced degree, that is also blessed in Divine Blessing Season Nine. Think big, and make those larger than life dreams a reality through embracing these opportunities and blessings. This is your time to embrace cultures, beliefs, and ideas that may be different from your own, opening you up to a world of opportunity!

Nurture the Blessings
Divine Timing Blessing – Season Nine
Focus on the Blessings

Focus on dreaming big, embracing learning, and growing in every way.

1. Focus on educational opportunities.
2. Go back to school to complete undergrad, master's, or an advanced degree.
3. Embrace international travel opportunities.
4. Get your book published.
5. Immigration status approved! Work to get a visa or green card for a foreign country.
6. Receive blessings working with companies overseas on an international level.
7. Work on a successful television or broadcast project.
8. Study a foreign language.
9. Be open to learning and growing.
10. Relocate to a new country.

Nurture the Blessings

Divine Timing Blessing – Season Ten

I Make My Mark in This World.

***You Are Blessed with Career Status
and Professional Achievement.***

Divine Time You Are in Now

Cancer (June 21 – July 22)
You will experience Divine Timing Blessing Season Ten during this time.

May 10, 2022, to October 28, 2022

December 20, 2022, to May 16, 2023

April 21, 2034, to April 29, 2035

Leo (July 23 – August 22)
You will experience Divine Timing Blessing Season Ten during this time.

May 16, 2023, to May 25, 2024

April 29, 2035, to May 9, 2036

April 13, 2047, to April 22, 2048

Virgo (August 23 – September 22)
You will experience Divine Timing Blessing Season Ten during this time.

May 25, 2024, to June 9, 2025

May 9, 2036, to May 23, 2037

April 22, 2048, to September 23, 2048

November 12, 2048, to May 5, 2049

Libra (September 23 – October 22)
You will experience Divine Timing Blessing Season Ten during this time.
June 9, 2025, to June 30, 2026
May 23, 2037, to June 12, 2038
September 23, 2048, to November 12, 2048
May 5, 2049, to September 27, 2049

Scorpio (October 23 – November 21)
You will experience Divine Timing Blessing Season Ten during this time.
June 30, 2026, to July 26, 2027
June 12, 2038, to November 16, 2038
January 16, 2039, to July 7, 2039

Sagittarius (November 22 – December 21)
You will experience Divine Timing Blessing Season Ten during this time.
July 26, 2027, to August 24, 2028
November 16, 2038, to January 16, 2039
July 7, 2039, to December 12, 2039
February 20, 2040, to August 5, 2040

Capricorn (December 22 – January 19)
You will experience Divine Timing Blessing Season Ten during this time.
August 24, 2028, to September 24, 2029
December 12, 2039, to February 20, 2040
August 5, 2040, to January 11, 2041
March 20, 2041, to September 5, 2041

Aquarius (January 20 – February 18)
You will experience Divine Timing Blessing Season Ten during this time.

September 24, 2029, to October 22, 2030
January 11, 2041, to March 20, 2041
September 5, 2041, to February 8, 2042
April 24, 2042, to October 4, 2042

Pisces (February 19 – March 20)

You will experience Divine Timing Blessing Season Ten during this time.

October 22, 2030, to November 15, 2031
February 8, 2042, to April 24, 2042
October 4, 2043, to June 9, 2043

Aries (March 21 – April 19)

You will experience Divine Timing Blessing Season Ten during this time.

November 15, 2031, to April 11, 2032
June 26, 2032, to November 29, 2032
March 1, 2043, to June 9, 2043
October 26, 2043, to March 15, 2044
August 9, 2044, to November 4, 2044

Taurus (April 20 – May 20)

You will experience Divine Timing Blessing Season Ten during this time.

December 19, 2020, to May 13, 2021
July 28, 2021, to December 28, 2021
April 11, 2032, to June 26, 2032
November 29, 2032, to April 14, 2033
September 12, 2033, to December 1, 2033
March 15, 2044, to August 9, 2044

Gemini (May 21 – June 20)

You will experience Divine Timing Blessing Season Ten during this time.

May 13, 2021, to July 28, 2021
December 28, 2021, to May 10, 2022
October 28, 2022, to December 20, 2022
April 14, 2033, to September 12, 2033
December 1, 2033, to April 21, 2034

"If you can dream it, you can do it."

— Walt Disney

"The way to get started is to quit talking and begin doing."

— Walt Disney

Nurture the Blessings
Divine Timing Blessing – Season Ten

When you are experiencing Divine Timing Blessing Season Ten, your career dreams are about to be realized! This is the time and season where all your past efforts are greatly rewarded. During Divine Blessing Season Ten, Teacher Jupiter glides over your life and sees what you are currently doing and how to enhance that experience for you with a big promotion, a new huge opportunity, or any career goal or dream that you have been putting intention and energy toward. From my experience, you have to be doing something toward your intention, even if it is small, for the Universe to see how to bless you. Yes, the Universe is intuitive and can bring a new opportunity that you never deemed possible.

However, to achieve the biggest career success during this season, you want to have planted some seeds that teacher Jupiter can rain down on and grow during this divine season. It's a scientific fact that it actually rains diamonds on Jupiter. So, ask yourself what diamonds would you like to see in your hat during Divine Timing Blessing Season Ten? If you're hoping for a promotion or to land a dream job or career opportunity, that can and will happen for you now. You must take action now, and Divine Timing Blessing Season Ten will answer with opportunity!

Where would you like to spend your energy? Your current job, a new direction, or a forgotten dream or goal? You may utilize this transit for all three, but make sure you use it for what you'd like to manifest in your life in the now or near future.

This blessing season looks at where you have placed your energy and intention over the course of the last 12 years. It asks you to choose where you'd like to be spending the next 12 years of your life or longer. If you answered doing exactly what you are doing now, that's fabulous—put all your energy and initiative into your current career or job, if that is fulfilling for you. If not, it's time to put energy and initiative into what you truly want to manifest in your life career-wise. For instance, if you're currently a CPA or accountant but you always wanted to be an artist and perhaps studied this topic and know you are talented or pursued art in the past but gave up because you wanted more job security, you can pick that up again and pursue it with full passion and gusto.

For example, when I went through this Jupiter transit, I was blessed in my job and had opportunities swirling about me in which I had a deep interest. I kept the job I was successful in but used my off hours to pursue my career passions and dreams. Opportunities came my way from the previous 12 years – things I had once loved, like music composition, writing this book, and broadcast opportunities I had pursued in the past. They all came knocking on my door as I pursued career growth and opportunity. Divine Timing Blessing Season Ten will now ask you what you desire to manifest in your career, and you must know the answer. Truly meditate on what you'd like to manifest with this transit. This blessing season will offer you opportunities that go beyond your wildest dreams. However, you must take action! Don't stand on the sidelines just waiting because this blessing season only lasts for 12 months and happens rarely, only every 12 years.

You may get a promotion, a new job that is a promotion, or a step up. If you've always wanted to start a business and have been tinkering around but were not fully committed, now is the time to act. Rare opportunities like this don't come along that often. If you're in a dead-end job that does not light your fire or make you feel good about yourself, it's time to embrace a new reality! You may have recently accepted a new job or career opportunity; if so, that job will be a blessing for you this year. You may be promoted within the year, or if you took a step up with this job opportunity, excellent!

This divine timing season can make you a master in your field and get you recognition from higher ups for a big promotion, landing the dream role or an exciting business deal!

I would suggest making preparations for this season. Even if you have a job that is not related to what you love to do, make sure you are putting intention and energy toward your true passion and gifts before this season arrives. Put some energy out there to show the Universe what you desire to accomplish in your career.

In the past — before I had this knowledge and was experiencing Divine Timing Blessing Season Ten —I had so many opportunities before me. The only problem was I was so distracted by the challenges in my life (which were in my love life at the time), I missed huge opportunities. Don't allow this to happen to you. While I was able to accomplish a lot during my Divine Blessing Season Ten, I would've accomplished much more if I would've had the knowledge that I'm giving you now.

Focus on the blessings in your life and starve the challenges. Put your complete focus on your current divine blessing season which is your career at this time. Note there will be a season for love, marriage, and everything else you'd like to occur in your life. The task is to focus on the here and now – the present moment where the wind is at your back, and that is your career. Also, being successful in your career can give you access to different types of people than you would have access to now. It's not saying that people will be attracted to you because of your success, but like attracts like. So, just know that love will happen for you in divine timing. But now is the time to focus on your career because, remember seasons change, and this season only happens every 12 years and lasts for a duration of 12 months. Divine Timing Season Ten is the season to manifest your heartfelt passions and career opportunities. Make it happen.

Nurture the Blessings Divine Timing Blessing – Season Ten Focus on the Blessings

This year, focus on your emerging career and really pursue your passion. The Universe asks, "What would you like to manifest in your career?" This year, you can make it happen.

1. Make a career vision board.
2. Meditate on what you want.
3. Pursue your passion.
4. Focus on manifesting your ideal career.
5. From Divine Timing Blessing Season Ten governing career and professional status, you can navigate
6. energy to love by working on a project with your spouse or significant other.
7. If single, new love can come through your career. However, focus on your career now. There will be times for new love in other blessing seasons.
8. Get in the training you need to move to the next level in your career.
9. Update your LinkedIn profile or resume.
10. Pursue any licenses that are needed in your field to propel you to the next level.
11. Ask yourself if you like your current career path; if not, change it.
12. Start your dream business.
13. Work with a career or business coach.
14. Plant seeds toward your future career goals.

<u>Nurture the Blessings</u>

Divine Timing Blessing – Season Eleven

*I Am Social, and I Am Blessed
with Great Connections.*

Divine Time You Are in Now

Gemini (May 21 - June 20)
You will experience Divine Timing Blessing Season Eleven during this time.
May 10, 2022, to October 28, 2022
December 20, 2022, to May 16, 2023
April 21, 2034, to April 29, 2035

Cancer (June 21 - July 22)
You will experience Divine Timing Blessing Season Eleven during this time.
May 16, 2023, to May 25, 2024
April 29, 2035, to May 9, 2036
April 13, 2047, to April 22, 2048

Leo (July 23 - August 22)
You will experience Divine Timing Blessing Season Eleven during this time.
May 25, 2024, to June 9, 2025
May 9, 2036, to May 23, 2037
April 22, 2048, to September 23, 2048
November 12, 2048, to May 5, 2049

Virgo (August 23 - September 22)
You will experience Divine Timing Blessing Season Eleven during this time.

June 9, 2025, to June 30, 2026
May 23, 2037, to June 12, 2038
September 23, 2048, to November 12, 2048
May 5, 2049, to September 27, 2049

Libra (September 23 - October 22)
You will experience Divine Timing Blessing Season Eleven during this time.
June 30, 2026, to July 26, 2027
June 12, 2038, to November 16, 2038
January 16, 2039, to July 7, 2039

Scorpio (October 23 - November 21)
You will experience Divine Timing Blessing Season Eleven during this time.
July 26, 2027, to August 24, 2028
November 16, 2038, to January 16, 2039
July 7, 2039, to December 12, 2039
February 20, 2040, to August 5, 2040

Sagittarius (November 22 - December 21)
You will experience Divine Timing Blessing Season Eleven during this time.
August 24, 2028, to September 24, 2029
December 12, 2039, to February 20, 2040
August 5, 2040, to January 11, 2041
March 20, 2041, to September 5, 2041

Capricorn (December 22 - January 19)
You will experience Divine Timing Blessing Season Eleven during this time.
September 24, 2029, to October 22, 2030
January 11, 2041, to March 20, 2041
September 5, 2041, to February 8, 2042
April 24, 2042, to October 4, 2042

Aquarius (January 20 - February 18)
You will experience Divine Timing Blessing Season Eleven during this time.

October 22, 2030, to November 15, 2031
February 8, 2042, to April 24, 2042
October 4, 2043, to June 9, 2043

Pisces (February 19 - March 20)
You will experience Divine Timing Blessing Season Eleven during this time.

November 15, 2031, to April 11, 2032
June 26, 2032, to November 29, 2032
March 1, 2043, to June 9, 2043
October 26, 2043, to March 15, 2044
August 9, 2044, to November 4, 2044

Aries (March 21 - April 19)
You will experience Divine Timing Blessing Season Eleven during this time.

December 19, 2020, to May 13, 2021
July 28, 2021, to December 28, 2021
April 11, 2032, to June 26, 2032
November 29, 2032, to April 14, 2033
September 12, 2033, to December 1, 2033
March 15, 2044, to August 9, 2044

Taurus (April 20 - May 20)
You will experience Divine Timing Blessing Season Eleven during this time.

May 13, 2021, to July 28, 2021
December 28, 2021, to May 10, 2022
October 28, 2022, to December 20, 2022
April 14, 2033, to September 12, 2033
December 1, 2033, to April 21, 2034

Nurture the Blessings
Divine Timing Blessing – Season Eleven

Divine Timing Blessing Season Eleven connects us to each other through what Dr. Gregg Braden calls, "The Divine Matrix." It is this interconnectivity of all things on the spiritual interconnected web and the connected web of online connectivity, as far as technology goes governing social media, also the connectivity of deep and meaningful friendships, humanity, and even the interconnectivity of astrology. Divine Timing Blessing Season Eleven encompasses astrology as an interconnected web of technology and information. It's interesting to note that astrological wisdom existed in many cultures before we had the ability of the interconnected web or the internet. Cultures such as Greece, Mesopotamia, Rome, African cultures including Egypt, India, China, Japanese culture, and even Tibetan culture, all had their own form of astrology.

Astrological knowledge is proof of a connected web of information that exists in the ether of consciousness.

Divine Timing Blessing Season Eleven will gift you with so many different aspects of interconnectivity. You can develop beautiful and amazing friendships, and your friends will be a source of joy and good for your life. You should meet and make new friends during this time which will season your life with excitement and joy. Career industries that are blessed during this season are technology, social media marketing and astrology. While this season brings friendships, it's not all about friendship. Since this same divine blessing season governs friends, a friend can make an introduction for you if you are wanting love and romance in your life.

Since this divine timing blessing season covers interconnectivity as well as the web and online activity, technology can also help you find love as long as you are not experiencing Divine Challenge Season Eleven at this time. Check the Navigate the Challenges chapter to check and see where your challenges are at this time. Proceed with caution — you can meet someone online or through a dating app, but use common sense and always meet in a public place. Drive your own vehicle and think about bringing a friend along, at least for the first meeting or two. While being smart and safe during this blessing season, you can attract love through friendship or technology. I failed to mention that a friend may also be a source of love at this time. If you are both single and there has been a connection between you, you may decide to take the next step during this time or, as stated before, your friend may actually introduce you to new love.

This is a great time to develop an app, build your business website, or start a social media campaign for success in your career. Although this house is not the house of career or the house of love, you can still utilize this divine season to nurture your blessings to manifest whatever you desire in life during whatever season you're in. You just have to be ready and stay in flow with the Universe, and apply the knowledge we've discussed in this chapter.

A wonderful part about this beautiful Divine Timing Blessing Season Eleven is that it can introduce you not only to friendships and love and new career opportunities but also to connections — powerful connections that can enhance your life in many ways. When speaking about love, friendships can enhance that for you by getting you out and about and making your life more social. This divine blessing season is also about humanity and volunteering. During this season, you will want to feel a connection to humanity, so you may volunteer in an area of service to humanity that is important to you and potentially join a nonprofit board. By joining this humanitarian cause, you will meet new friends who will add to your life in many of the ways we've already discussed in this chapter. Utilize Divine Timing Blessing Season Eleven to bring about change in your life through connectivity, humanity, and deep, meaningful friendships. Focus on the blessings, and enjoy Divine Timing Season Eleven.

I think we should summarize this chapter because Divine Timing Blessing Season Eleven covers so much. So, in summary, friends will be a big blessing this year and greatly nurture your life. Life will be such a peach with social groups, friends, associations, and clubs. If you have found it difficult to meet friends due to relocation or a move or just have not had the focus, this year you will meet friends that will last a lifetime! This same house of friends also governs over social media like Facebook, Twitter, and technology.

If you work in technology, you may come up with an amazing new app this year, or if not in technology, you may partner with someone in technology to do so. If in digital marketing or if you have a brand, you have developed or are developing, digital marketing will work wonders for you and your brand. Be sure to invest in SEO and a digital brand specialist. Astrology is also ruled by this same house, so if you have an interest in astrology, by all means, take a class, or start to learn on your own. This is an excellent year to also get involved with a nonprofit board that will lend you wonderful professional contacts and friendships. Choose a nonprofit that you have a natural interest in investing your time and resources so you can make a difference. This will insure you meet like-minded souls who will be a blessing to your path. This is also a wonderful time to promote what you do with a new website, business, or brand-focused Facebook, Instagram, or Twitter page.

There are so many areas of life this Divine Timing Blessing Season Eleven can deliver for you, from career and social life to love! Have a friend make an introduction for you! Also, online dating is found in Divine Timing Blessing Season Eleven, and it can bode well for you. Although online dating has changed quite a bit and you must be smart and careful, during this season, it can be extremely lucky for you! As said before, always meet in a public place and take safety precautions. However, online dating or a friend's introduction can lead to long-term love! Friends will offer so much joy, married or single. Enjoy a couple's night out and just more social fun with your spouse! It's all so exciting! Welcome to your year of social enjoyment when even business deals will be accomplished while having fun! What a year for wonderful friendships! You truly have a blessed year in store! Life will start to feel lighter and more joyful!

Nurture the Blessings Divine Timing Blessing – Season Eleven Focus on the Blessings

Focus on creating meaningful friendships, social networks, social media marketing, and emerging technology for business.

1. Friendships
2. Creating a fulfilling social life
3. Social media marketing
4. Technology
5. Develop an app
6. Study astrology
7. Get elected to a top board
8. Promote your business digitally
9. Design your website
10. Create a winning marketing plan

<u>Nurture the Blessings</u>

Divine Timing Blessing – Season Twelve

*I Am the Muse. I Am Blessed with Divine
Wellness and an Inspired Vision.*

Divine Time You Are in Now

Taurus (April 20 - May 20)
**You will experience Divine Timing Blessing Season Twelve during
this time.**
May 10, 2022, to October 28, 2022
December 20, 2022, to May 16, 2023
April 21, 2034, to April 29, 2035

Gemini (May 21 - June 20)
**You will experience Divine Timing Blessing Season Twelve during
this time.**
May 16, 2023, to May 25, 2024
April 29, 2035, to May 9, 2036
April 13, 2047, to April 22, 2048

Cancer (June 21 - July 22)
**You will experience Divine Timing Blessing Season Twelve during
this time.**
May 25, 2024, to June 9, 2025
May 9, 2036, to May 23, 2037
April 22, 2048, to September 23, 2048
November 12, 2048, to May 5, 2049

Leo (July 23 - August 22)
**You will experience Divine Timing Blessing Season Twelve during
this time.**

June 9, 2025, to June 30, 2026
May 23, 2037, to June 12, 2038
September 23, 2048, to November 12, 2048
May 5, 2049, to September 27, 2049

Virgo (August 23 - September 22)
You will experience Divine Timing Blessing Season Twelve during this time.
June 30, 2026, to July 26, 2027
June 12, 2038, to November 16, 2038
January 16, 2039, to July 7, 2039

Libra (September 23 - October 22)
You will experience Divine Timing Blessing Season Twelve during this time.
July 26, 2027, to August 24, 2028
November 16, 2038, to January 16, 2039
July 7, 2039, to December 12, 2039
February 20, 2040, to August 5, 2040

Scorpio (October 23 - November 21)
You will experience Divine Timing Blessing Season Twelve during this time.
August 24, 2028, to September 24, 2029
December 12, 2039, to February 20, 2040
August 5, 2040, to January 11, 2041
March 20, 2041, to September 5, 2041

Sagittarius (November 22 - December 21)
You will experience Divine Timing Blessing Season Twelve during this time.
September 24, 2029, to October 22, 2030
January 11, 2041, to March 20, 2041
September 5, 2041, to February 8, 2042
April 24, 2042, to October 4, 2042

Capricorn (December 22 - January 19)
You will experience Divine Timing Blessing Season Twelve during this time.

October 22, 2030, to November 15, 2031

February 8, 2042, to April 24, 2042

October 4, 2043, to June 9, 2043

Aquarius (January 20 - February 18)
You will experience Divine Timing Blessing Season Twelve during this time.

November 15, 2031, to April 11, 2032

June 26, 2032, to November 29, 2032

March 1, 2043, to June 9, 2043

October 26, 2043, to March 15, 2044

August 9, 2044, to November 4, 2044

Pisces (February 19 - March 20)
You will experience Divine Timing Blessing Season Twelve during this time.

December 19, 2020, to May 13, 2021

July 28, 2021, to December 28, 2021

April 11, 2032, to June 26, 2032

November 29, 2032, to April 14, 2033

September 12, 2033, to December 1, 2033

March 15, 2044, to August 9, 2044

Aries (March 21 - April 19)
You will experience Divine Timing Blessing Season Twelve during this time.

May 13, 2021, to July 28, 2021

December 28, 2021, to May 10, 2022

October 28, 2022, to December 20, 2022

April 14, 2033, to September 12, 2033

December 1, 2033, to April 21, 2034

Nurture the Blessings
Divine Timing Blessing –
Season Twelve

When the stars twinkle brightly and you are in Divine Timing Blessing Season Twelve, you engage with spirit. It is the time of an inspired spiritual wellness journey. Everyone's journey is different, but you will no doubt create some sort of a spiritual practice that involves body, spirit, and mental wellness. Even if you don't consider yourself spiritual, you will have your own spiritual path that has meaning to you, and at the end of this divine season, you may in fact become your own version of spirituality.

This divine blessing season protects you with unseen forces, although we are always engaged and protected by unseen forces simply by asking for help. When you're experiencing Divine Timing Blessings Season Twelve, you are experiencing divine inspiration of spirit, extra guidance, and divine protection. You will also experience a divine inspiration of art. Life should take on an inspired tone. Divine Timing Blessing Season Twelve encompasses the arts, including music, film, and visual arts. Art is life, and life is art. It's a wonderful time to craft a beautiful story that will include wellness practices that benefit the body, the spirit, and the mind.

When I experienced Divine Timing Season Twelve, I had just started my journey in holistic health. I had always been attracted to the spirit world and the beauty of all it encompasses. After going through such pain in relationships, I particularly noticed the spirit world was always light to my path and joy to my spirit. Even in the darkest moments, it provided light that pierced the darkness.

I enjoyed learning about botanical medicine, herbal medicine, holistic spirituality, and all forms of divine wellness. I had always studied astrology, even though I was frightened to study it with my Christian upbringing.

I always had a natural understanding of it, like knowledge passed down from a past life. When I was a child, I wrote a play called *Rags to Jupiter,* and it was shocking that this little girl from London was rescued by planet Jupiter. I had no knowledge in this life that Jupiter was the planet of blessings and good fortune. However, Jupiter rescued this British little girl who thought she had to steal for food. She was living in the streets of London, and Jupiter made her realize her place in this world. This little girl was actually a divine princess, a queen with rulership and power, and she needed to recognize it. So, the queen of Jupiter took the child to her planet (which is Jupiter) to show her the kingdom and what she could accomplish. I believe I wrote that story when I was seven or eight years old. However, the spirit world was gifting me knowledge that I could not yet understand. Jupiter is, in fact, the planet that actually governs over blessings. You can find more information about that in the index.

However, I shared that story (which you also find in my forward) to give an account as to the power of Divine Timing Blessing Season Twelve. Spirit will give you beautiful dreams and reveal to you more of who you are. This season is not just about divine spirit. It is about crafting a wellness journey. My experience with Divine Timing Blessing Season Twelve has had a diverse array of manifestations in my life. I studied holistic health independently before I decided to embark on my journey to graduate school at Georgian Court University, studying holistic health formally. Georgian Court University's Holistic Health Program was dynamic and magical and one of the few accredited programs in holistic health. I felt like I was attending Hogwarts University.

I had always studied astrology and sought out a spiritual path. That's written in my birth chart. I've grown throughout the years, and my path has changed and become richer and all-encompassing and less about religion and more about love and spirit. My mom actually always taught us as children that it was not about religion but about love. Although my mom raised us Christian because her father was a Baptist pastor and we went to Catholic school, when I would bring home topics we learned about relating to judgment and religion, my mom would always bring it back to the spiritual realm saying God is love. I'm sure that's greatly contributed to my spiritual walk today.

This new holistic health journey involving botanical medicine, nutrition, and herbal medicine, also came about due to my mom. This journey started when my mom was having issues with beta blockers and her blood pressure and some other issues, and I wanted to find a natural solution for my mom's well-being. I was conveniently living with my mother at home at the time, and we invested in many herbal remedies until I found the right mix for my mom. I noticed that the herbal and botanical medicine I found had 10 benefits as opposed to prescription medicine which would have one specific benefit but then 10 scary and horrible side effects.

My mom's condition improved, and she had no side effects. I started to see wellness as a creative force of energy. My mom's improvement was like a miracle, all based on botanical and herbal medicine.

That journey led to me to pursue my graduate degree in holistic health which was one of my favorite seasons of life. As this season of spirituality, self-knowledge and self-awareness led me to all the other blessings I experienced, from meeting my husband, to this current book I'm writing, to all of the experiences and the magic and synchronicity I had when I moved to Red Bank, New Jersey, to attend graduate school (that story is shared in Divine Timing Blessing Season One).

All of the movement I had in life started in the spiritual world. Beyond that, there are so many stories of spirit interacting within my life that I don't know if there's enough time to put it all in this book or in this chapter.

However, I want you to get the knowledge and the point about the divine and beautiful changes that can happen in your life during Divine Timing Blessing Season Twelve.

So, we've covered a bit about spirituality, body, spirit, and mental wellness. To touch on that I would say it's an excellent time for you to craft your own wellness plan, either with or without a coach. Just get started. Your wellness plan may include meditative walks, Pilates, tai chi, yoga, meditation, shamanistic journeying, sound baths, learning about botanical medicine, learning about herbs, learning about your spirit guides, and mindful nutrition for wellness, learning about food as medicine and reading spiritual books or anything that enriches your mind, spirit, and body.

From the inspired and artistic standpoint if you are an artist working in the industries of film or music, this is an excellent time to create. You will have the focus and the spiritual help to create magnificent pieces of art, screenplays, films, fashion design, photography, and visual arts in any form.

Also, during Divine Timing Blessings Season Twelve, you are not only protected by unseen forces in the spiritual world, you are protected by secret VIPs in your life. This divine season sets you up for success for the next divine blessing season after twelve which is the Divine Timing Blessing Season One. That season is a season of becoming. However, this Divine Timing Blessing Season Twelve brings forth the magic, the inspiration, and the wellness you need to thrive in the next divine timing season. This current season you are in, Divine Timing Blessing Season Twelve, will deliver the healing you need for your body, spirit, and mind as secret forces work to help you. If you work in the medical field or in healing arts, this can be a blessing and also provide you opportunities in this field because this divine blessing season also governs hospitals and healing.

As we discussed, Divine Blessing Season Twelve encompasses art, spirituality, film, fashion design, and music. Spiritual forces will be very relevant in moving your life forward in this realm as well. Divine Timing Blessing Season Twelve does not govern over religion like the Divine Timing Blessing Season Nine, which is greatly about discussions and expansion of ideas and formal religion. No, this Divine Blessing Season Twelve is when you would go to a spa retreat, yoga retreat, or speak with a shaman or a therapist for healing. It is also the house where you would produce art, an art gallery, film, or music. This is also a great time to work in solitude, immersed in writing, meditation, and studying spiritual topics ... these types of focuses should all be very helpful now.

Another great wonder about Divine Blessing Season Twelve is that VIPs, in the background or in secret, will be working behind the scenes to bless and promote you. This is the year to embrace namaste, "peace be still," and the beauty of the spirit. If you're not into yoga, embrace Qigong or tai chi, which are moving meditations. Through embracing spirit, you will bring your best self to the forefront, for your benefit and the benefit of others. If you've wanted to write about spiritual topics, let this blessing season help in that area of working diligently alone in peace and stillness. You'll see growth and the ability to manifest your dreams through focus, visualization, and determination. This will be a year of spiritual growth and healing that your mind, soul, and body have been waiting for! Embrace the blessings! Remember, wherever you are experiencing your Navigate the Challenges season, currently revealed in the Navigate the Challenges chapter, create the best life and focus on and nurture the blessings that would be Divine Timing Blessing Season Twelve currently. It's time to nurture your body, spirit, and mental wellness, creating the magic and light that will pierce any darkness to create and manifest the life of your dreams.

Nurture the Blessings Divine Timing Blessing – Season Twelve Focus on the Blessings

I invest in my own wellness and embark on a spiritual journey.

1. Focus on the Blessings of Divine Timing Season Twelve; starve the challenges.
2. Spirituality
3. Self-Care
4. Healing
5. Speaking with a therapist
6. Studying a spiritual topic
7. Working in solitude
8. Meditate, journal.
9. Develop an appreciation of art, film, and music.
10. Embark on a spiritual and healing journey.
11. Compose music, design fashion, write a screenplay, create visual art, photography and cinematography.
12. Create a wellness plan that encompasses body, spirit, and mind.

Chapter 14 – The Power of Divine Timing: Navigate the Twelve Challenge Seasons

Without knowing any details, I'm certain you are already aware of where you're experiencing the biggest challenges in your life, whether that's a relationship, marriage, your children, finances, career goals, your job, or your health and well-being.

We generally know exactly where we're experiencing our greatest challenges. Our challenges tend to be much louder than our blessings. In essence, they are the squeaky wheel. Our blessings are much softer. They tend to hide out in the background.

Blessings are simply not as loud as challenges as they are not requiring anything of us. Challenges require a response and sometimes a very swift one. Many times, we have become accustomed to the presence of our blessings, and we ignore and starve them. Due to the fact, our blessings are not posing a problem, they don't tend to take a leading role in our lives.

Our blessings don't ask for attention or look for tending or nurturing. However, what happens if you don't water a plant? It withers and dies. If you don't feed and nurture your little one, they will get sick. The same goes for nurturing the seeds of good in our lives.

We have been taught to really focus on our problems in this current society. We are very problem-solver focused. However, I invite you to consider a new way of thinking and living. If you master it, it can simply change the outcomes in your life to be exceedingly positive. It's imperative to nurture the things in our lives that are nurturing us.

We are often taught to really focus on problems and solve them in our own lives and in the lives of our loved ones. We've been taught this way of thinking and dealing with challenges since grade school. It's not that problems should be ignored, and we'll speak about that a bit later in the book; it's just that we should invest our greatest intention and energy in what is currently blessing, feeding, and nurturing us. The divine timing challenge seasons are divided into 12 sectors that correspond to different areas of our life, ranging from career and finance to love and marriage to health and well-being and more. In astrology, the term "house" is utilized to describe these sectors or areas of life. For the purpose of *The Power of Divine Timing* and the goal of understanding *The Power of Divine Timing Method*, we have simplified the astrological terms to help readers more easily digest the information, thus creating more rapid change in their lives.

In this chapter, we will recognize the twelve divine challenge seasons. We want to acknowledge them yet give them as minimal intention and energy as possible. Many times, the cause for incorrect investments of energy is people simply don't know where to focus their energy. They have starved the blessings so much they can't locate them. Their challenges have screamed so loud at them that the small voice of blessing, which is kind, supportive, and nurturing, can no longer be recognized. We get into this topic more in the Nurture the Blessings section of this book. In the meantime, let's focus on navigating the challenges. This section of the book has corresponding dates for each Sun sign and rising sign for each divine timing challenge season.

For example, when you get to the chapter of Navigate the Challenges – Divine Timing Challenge Season One, you should locate the dates of your Sun sign and rising sign. Take notes as to when you are going through a specific challenge and highlight the blessing season you are experiencing at the time. This is the method to create the success you desire. Simply focus your intention on the blessing season more than your challenge season. This takes a lot of practice, but if you master this skill, it can assist you with manifesting an amazing life in flow with the divine timing of the Universe.

<u>Navigate the Challenges</u>

Divine Timing Challenge – Season One

Your Vision of Self Is Being Challenged.

Divine Time You Are in Now

Aries (March 21st - April 19)
You will experience Divine Timing Challenge Season One during this time.
May 24, 2025, to September 1, 2025
February 13, 2026, to April 12, 2028

Taurus (April 20 - May 20)
You will experience Divine Timing Challenge Season One during this time.
April 12, 2028, to May 31, 2030

Gemini (May 21 - June 20)
You will experience Divine Timing Challenge Season One during this time.
May 31, 2030, to July 13, 2032

Cancer (June 21 - July 22)
You will experience Divine Timing Challenge Season One during this time.
July 13, 2032, to August 26, 2034
February 15, 2035, to May 11, 2035

Leo (July 23 - August 22)
You will experience Divine Timing Challenge Season One during this time.
August 26, 2034, to February 15, 2035

May 11, 2035, to October 16, 2036
February 11, 2037, to July 6, 2037

Virgo (August 23 - September 22)
You will experience Divine Timing Challenge Season One during this time.
October 16, 2036, to February 11, 2037
July 6, 2037, to September 5, 2039

Libra (September 23 - October 22)
You will experience Divine Timing Challenge Season One during this time.
September 5, 2039, to November 11, 2041
June 21, 2042, to July 14, 2042

Scorpio (October 23 - November 21)
You will experience Divine Timing Challenge Season One during this time.
July 14, 2042, to February 21, 2044
March 25, 2044, to October 31, 2044

Sagittarius (November 22 - December 21)
You will experience Divine Timing Challenge Season One during this time.
February 21, 2044, to March 25, 2044
October 31, 2044, to January 24, 2047
July 10, 2047, to October 22, 2047

Capricorn (December 22 - January 19)
You will experience Divine Timing Challenge Season One during this time.
December 19, 2017, to March 21, 2020
July 1, 2020, to December 17, 2020
January 24, 2047, to July 10, 2047
October 22, 2047, to January 21, 2050

Aquarius (January 20 - February 18)
You will experience Divine Timing Challenge Season One during this time.

March 21, 2020, to July 1, 2020

December 17, 2020, to March 7, 2023

Pisces (February 19 - March 20)
You will experience Divine Timing Challenge Season One during this time.

March 7, 2023, to May 24, 2025

September 1, 2025, to February 13, 2026

Navigate the Challenges
Divine Timing Challenge – Season One

The time you are in now – Divine Timing Challenge Season One is a notable time when Saturn transits your first house or sector of life, governing "self", that is Saturn's current placement on your Sun or ascendant; it is a true time of reckoning or rising to the occasion. It's a time when all lessons are assimilating, and Saturn challenges you to become who you say you are or who you say you want to be. You say you want to be the best, you want to create a business, you want to move cross country. Now is the time of reckoning to become who you say you are. When Saturn transits your first house, that is to say your sun sign or your rising sign, you may feel overwhelmed. A sense of lack can make you feel you have not accomplished enough. Self-doubt can loom or a feeling of being limited. A feeling that you have not accomplished or become who you set out to be. However, you can also utilize this force to achieve greatness by having mercy upon yourself and recognizing what you like about your life and what you don't.

It's a time of re-creation; you will step up to the plate of responsibility. When Saturn gives you Divine Timing Challenge Season One, your only goal is to become. You may feel like your entire life needs a makeover. The challenge is to give yourself the opportunity to become – to allow yourself to become.

When you are experiencing Divine Timing Challenge One, you will encounter challenges affecting your sense of self, your life and how you show up in the world, in essence. It's a time of reckoning. It's a time of becoming the person you've said you've always wanted to be. The Universe wants you to give your very best in every way toward how you show up in this world.

With this specific divine timing challenge, you must step up to the plate with complete responsibility. You may be feeling a lack of understanding of your place in this world or confidence toward what you want to achieve. This challenge, Divine Timing Challenge Season One, really is dependent on you and how you show up for yourself. With Teacher Saturn in this sector of your life, Divine Timing Challenge Season One, on the challenging side of things, you may feel like life is not working for you – like you don't understand how to make things work or like you need a complete life change.

This time can be a very pleasant time if you put yourself in the right state of mind to achieve your goals and if you are clear on what you want to manifest in the world. Even if you are unclear, this transit will be a good teacher as to what is needed to create a life that is pleasing to you.

In my time of doing hundreds of charts for clients, I have also observed when Teacher Saturn transits your sun sign or ascendant sign which is Divine Timing Challenge Season One. You in essence become Teacher Saturn. You will represent that transit of Teacher Saturn for anyone's life you come in contact with for a season of time and how you impact their chart.

Let's say you are in Divine Timing Challenge Season One which is a transit of Saturn to the first sector of your house of self. Let's say, for example, during that time, your child has a lesson in Divine Timing Challenge Season Four, ruling parents. At that time, your relationship may become challenging with your child as you represent the planet of challenges.

Your relationship may not be a challenge for you, but with you representing challenges with the planet teacher of challenges and Saturn being on your sun or ascendant sign, you will become, in essence, that teacher. Whether you are right or wrong, the lessons you are teaching your child as part of the assignment of that time is for you to become the challenge. With Master Teacher Saturn and also with Master Teacher Jupiter, when we have a transit to our house of self, we become that teacher.

This is why it is imperative when you have this experience of Divine Timing Challenge Season One, that you become your best version of yourself. It is not only for your good but for the good of others you come in contact with.

If you do rise to the occasion of the moment, you will be rewarded greatly by Master Teacher Saturn during Challenge Season One. Teacher Saturn respects responsibility, taking responsibility, following the proper methods and procedures for success, taking the time to do things correctly, honesty, integrity, and following proven measures and tried-and-true methods toward your endeavor for success.

During this season, you also want to pay close attention to the area and placement of where your blessings are coming. That timing can be found in the Nurture the Blessings chapter.

Lessons You Are Learning Divine Timing Challenge - Season One

- Follow proven methods and procedures for success.
- Take responsibility.
- Make plans for what you would like to achieve and follow them.
- Have integrity with every interaction.
- Become the best version of yourself.
- Take action toward goals for your life.
- Be kind to yourself and attend to your wellness.
- Nurture and locate your blessings.
- Spend as much time as possible during this 2½-3-year season in the Nurture the Blessings area of your chart in which Jupiter is transiting during this divine time.

<u>Navigate the Challenges</u>

Divine Timing Challenge – Season Two

Your Earned Income and Financial Stability, and What You Value Is Being Challenged.

Time You Are in Now

Pisces (February 19 - March 20)
You will experience Divine Timing Challenge Season Two during this time.
May 24, 2025, to September 1, 2025
February 13, 2026, to April 12, 2028

Aries (March 21st - April 19)
You will experience Divine Timing Challenge Season Two during this time.
April 12, 2028, to May 31, 2030

Taurus (April 20 - May 20)
You will experience Divine Timing Challenge Season Two during this time.
May 31, 2030, to July 13, 2032

Gemini (May 21 - June 20)
You will experience Divine Timing Challenge Season Two during this time.
July 13, 2032, to August 26, 2034
February 15, 2035, to May 11, 2035

Cancer (June 21 - July 22)
You will experience Lesson Plan Two during this time.
August 26, 2034, to February 15, 2035

May 11, 2035, to October 16, 2036
February 11, 2037, to July 6, 2037

Leo (July 23 - August 22)
You will experience Divine Timing Challenge Season Two during this time.
October 16, 2036, to February 11, 2037
July 6, 2037, to September 5, 2039

Virgo (August 23 - September 22)
You will experience Divine Timing Challenge Season Two during this time.
September 5, 2039, to November 11, 2041
June 21, 2042, to July 14, 2042

Libra (September 23 - October 22)
You will experience Divine Timing Challenge Season Two during this time.
July 14, 2042, to February 21, 2044
March 25, 2044, to October 31, 2044

Scorpio (October 23 - November 21)
You will experience Divine Timing Challenge Season Two during this time.
February 21, 2044, to March 25, 2044
October 31, 2044, to January 24, 2047
July 10, 2047, to October 22, 2047

Sagittarius (November 22 - December 21)
You will experience Divine Timing Challenge Season Two during this time.
December 19, 2017, to March 21, 2020
July 1, 2020, to December 17, 2020
January 24, 2047, to July 10, 2047
October 22, 2047, to January 21, 2050

Capricorn (December 22 - January 19)
You will experience Divine Timing Challenge Season Two during this time.

March 21, 2020, to July 1, 2020

December 17, 2020, to March 7, 2023

Aquarius (January 20 - February 18)
You will experience Divine Timing Challenge Season Two during this time.

March 7, 2023, to May 24, 2025

September 1, 2025, to February 13, 2026

Navigate the Challenges
Divine Timing Challenge –
Season Two

When you are in Divine Timing Challenge Season Two, your income is generally less and a bit more difficult to earn. You may be working a job where you signed on and took less pay than what you are worth. You may be working and earning an income in a way that does not truly bring you joy or peace.

Work will be a bit scarce, or if it's plentiful, raises may seem delayed if you work for an employer. And if you are self-employed, the clientele may be difficult, delay paying your invoices, or other delays may occur that cause your income to be less than usual. By looking ahead while staying present in the moment, we can plan for such times. Once Saturn, the planet teacher, is transiting the sector of your life which I call Divine Timing Season Two, you must adequately prepare for it.

Similar to the farmer who stores up for the winter knowing there will be a time of scarcity, it may seem you go from feast to famine rather quickly. This season is teaching you the value of money, of planting seeds and saving up and harvesting, and the value of working in creative ways to be financially stable and happy. Instead of going out to restaurants often, perhaps you spend more time at home preparing affordable meals and having family and guests over. You save money where you can while still seeing that life can offer you joy and happiness, even in a season of financial lack.

I have experienced this myself in my life, and it's not fun. However, this transit teaches you how to be wise with money, so when you do have plenty of financial means, you remember this time of lack and are able to adjust your spending and resolve your earned income accordingly. It's also important to note since this challenge is in reference to earned income, it also relates to our time as being valuable. This transit also asks us what we value. In many "earned income" or work situations, we trade time for money. This time-for-money sacrifice may require travel time away from family, long hours, or other sacrifices of our time like working nights and/or weekends. Every work situation generally requires some sort of trade-off or sacrifice for financial benefit.

When we are in this Challenge Season Two, the Universe asks us what we value. I had a dear colleague of mine who worked tirelessly for a company. The company demanded to be first as this was the "cost" of success – first above family, first above your spouse, and first above your own well-being. This schedule taxed his relationship with his spouse as there was no balance. He clearly had to choose his employer over his family. Sacrificing one for the other. This is not to say you should not have to sacrifice anything for a work situation as that is unrealistic.

Even in a perfect entrepreneurial venture, there will be needed sacrifices of your time. However, in this lesson in Divine Timing Challenge Season Two, we are also learning the value of our time. In this transit, you may find you need to create more balance in regards to other areas of life you might value more than money while remaining responsible and vigilant toward your financial well-being.

By utilizing The Power of Divine Timing, specifically, you can prepare for such seasons. When reading Divine Timing Challenge Season Two, just find your corresponding dates for your sun sign and rising and note those dates, so you can make wise choices and decisions moving forward and preparing for that time.

The planets are always moving, so this assures us that time will change and your timing for financial success will occur again. However, to make it to that time, we have to go with the flow while learning life's lessons and mastering them.

I had a client who had Saturn transiting this part of her chart. She was in Divine Timing Challenge Season Two, navigating the challenges which is a Saturn transit by Teacher Saturn to the second house (or sector) of earned income. She had challenges here but had the planet of blessings, Jupiter, in her house of real estate and home, representing home, parents, real estate, and construction. She went into real estate and was very successful and was able to find success navigating past this divine timing challenge season.

For example, you may instead be blessed at the same time in the Nurture the Blessing section with the gift of Divine Season Three which gives you the ability to write and develop concepts that will reward you in the future.

This may be the time that you write your hit song, your *New York Times* bestselling book, or another communication project that lends itself toward a season of financial blessing for you in the future. Just remember, everything is working together to help you on your path toward success. We want to starve the challenge by nurturing where you're experiencing the wind at your back and ease during this season, and that would be whatever divine season of blessing you are in which you can locate timing wise in the Nurture the Blessing section of this book.

Lessons You Are Learning Divine Timing Challenge – Season Two

- How to appreciate earned income
- Stretching a dollar
- Saving for a rainy day
- The value of money
- How to thrive during a season of lack
- To appreciate income-earning opportunities when you have them
- The value of resources and how to utilize them
- How to be creative with living well on less
- The gift of finding your path potentially in another field to make money
- Developing wisdom around what we value

<u>Navigate the Challenges</u>

Divine Timing Challenge – Season Three

Your Communication and Sibling/Cousin Relationships Are Being Challenged.

Divine Time You Are in Now

Aquarius (January 20 - February 18)
You will experience Divine Timing Challenge Season Three during this time.

May 24, 2025, to September 1, 2025

February 13, 2026, to April 12, 2028

Pisces (February 19 - March 20)
You will experience Divine Timing Challenge Season Three during this time.

April 12, 2028, to May 31, 2030

Aries (March 21st - April 19)
You will experience Divine Timing Challenge Season Three during this time.

May 31, 2030, to July 13, 2032

Taurus (April 20 - May 20)
You will experience Divine Timing Challenge Season Three during this time.

July 13, 2032, to August 26, 2034

February 15, 2035, to May 11, 2035

Gemini (May 21 - June 20)
You will experience Divine Timing Challenge Season Three during this time.

August 26, 2034, to February 15, 2035
May 11, 2035, to October 16, 2036
February 11, 2037, to July 6, 2037

Cancer (June 21 - July 22)
You will experience Divine Timing Challenge Season Three during this time.
October 16, 2036, to February 11, 2037
July 6, 2037, to September 5, 2039

Leo (July 23 - August 22)
You will experience Divine Timing Challenge Season Three during this time.
September 5, 2039, to November 11, 2041
June 21, 2042, to July 14, 2042

Virgo (August 23 - September 22)
You will experience Divine Timing Challenge Season Three during this time.
July 14, 2042, to February 21, 2044
March 25, 2044, to October 31, 2044

Libra (September 23 - October 22)
You will experience Divine Timing Challenge Season Three during this time.
February 21, 2044, to March 25, 2044
October 31, 2044, to January 24, 2047
July 10, 2047, to October 22, 2047

Scorpio (October 23 - November 21)
You will experience Divine Timing Challenge Season Three during this time.
December 19, 2017, to March 21, 2020
July 1, 2020, to December 17, 2020

January 24, 2047, to July 10, 2047
October 22, 2047, to January 21, 2050

Sagittarius (November 22 - December 21)
You will experience Divine Timing Challenge Season Three during this time.
March 21, 2020, to July 1, 2020
December 17, 2020, to March 7, 2023

Capricorn (December 22 - January 19)
You will experience Divine Timing Challenge Season Three during this time.
March 7, 2023, to May 24, 2025
September 1, 2025, to February 13, 2026

Navigate the Challenges
Divine Timing Challenge – Season Three

When you're in Divine Timing Challenge Season Three, this area covers siblings, cousins, communication, transport, and vehicles. This divine season speaks to all forms of communication which include writing, speaking, writing or composing music, and contracts. This season also includes your neighborhood. It rules how we interact and think and communicate with others. That could be your neighbors, a presentation at work, or even how we interact with our siblings which is also under this sector. And because this challenge season also rules vehicles, this is not a good time to purchase a car. If you need to purchase a car, purchase a car after this season or before the season. Check when you are experiencing Divine Timing Season Three to purchase a vehicle, if possible. With this season of challenges in this area, also make sure you invest in a maintenance program for your car and get it maintained often, if possible, and invest in a roadside assistance service like Triple A (AAA).

During this time, you may be concerned about the well-being of a sibling, or you may have a falling out with a sibling. You may notice that your communication style may be challenged, and you may even have some challenges with neighbors. During this time, you may decide that you want to move neighborhoods, based on your interaction with neighbors.

As far as learning and communicating, there are many different ways Divine Season Challenge Three can affect you. Saturn is a very focused planet. We are tracking Saturn with each challenge and how it affects us in each area of life and then learning to starve the challenge and nurture the area of life that is blessing us.

When Saturn is in your communication sector, you may find communication a bit more challenging. You may find you experience writer's block if you're a writer, or you may completely change your communication style. Although Saturn is the planet of challenges, teaching in this house may also give you more focus toward a writing project or toward a communication project involving public speaking presentations and any form of communication. However, during Challenge Season Three with teacher Saturn, you may feel like writing is not a joy, and it may not give you pleasure.

Learning new topics, public speaking, and making presentations may be a source of stress at this time as well. I suggest you are thoughtful about what you say before you say it when communicating with those you love during this time, specifically siblings. Also, be thoughtful when communicating with neighbors and co-workers. Before you send an email, reread and check the communication. If someone upsets you, like a neighbor or co-worker, slow down and maybe meditate for a moment before responding.

I feel relationships with our siblings and cousins are valuable as we have often, in most cases, experienced growing up together and had similar experiences throughout childhood. Regarding siblings and cousins during this time, it's important that you be the best version of yourself, giving assistance to a sibling if needed while still maintaining some boundaries for your own well-being.

I am very close with my siblings and thank God for that. When I encountered Saturn in this house, two of my siblings were not getting along at all, and one of my siblings was going through a very tough time. If your sibling needs you during this time in any way and you value the relationship, you should be there as much as possible in any way you can.

If you're noticing that you're not getting along with a sibling, take the high road as much as possible. If you're not getting along, perhaps attempt to see things from your sibling's point of view as much as possible and send them as much light and love as you can.

However, if your sibling is toxic to you and your life, you will have to create healthy boundaries while still keeping the relationship intact. This divine challenge season is determined to teach us the value of excellent communication skills and even overcoming challenges in that arena as well as the challenges in the arena of sibling relationships.

Lessons You Are Learning Divine Timing Challenge - Season Three

- Navigating communication issues
- Learning what does work and what doesn't work in communication
- Navigating challenges in sibling relationships
- Being there for your siblings and cousins, if needed
- Learning the power of focus in all communication styles
- The value of interactions with others
- The value of every communication style
- Approaches that work in presentations and approaches that don't work
- The value of your siblings and cousins
- The value of honing and developing your communication skills as a whole
- The power of words and how words can be a blessing or destructive to your life and the lives of others

<u>Navigate the Challenges</u>

Divine Timing Challenge – Season Four

Your Sense of Security Is Being Challenged In Home, Family, Parents, and Real Estate.

Divine Time You Are in Now

Capricorn (December 22 - January 19)
You will experience Divine Timing Challenge Season Four during this time.

May 24, 2025, to September 1, 2025

February 13, 2026, to April 12, 2028

Aquarius (January 20 - February 18)
You will experience Divine Timing Challenge Season Four during this time.

April 12, 2028, to May 31, 2030

Pisces (February 19 - March 20)
You will experience Divine Timing Challenge Season Four during this time.

May 31, 2030, to July 13, 2032

Aries (March 21st - April 19)
You will experience Divine Timing Challenge Season Four during this time.

July 13, 2032, to August 26, 2034

February 15, 2035, to May 11, 2035

Taurus (April 20 - May 20)
You will experience Divine Timing Challenge Season Four during this time.

August 26, 2034, to February 15, 2035
May 11, 2035, to October 16, 2036
February 11, 2037, to July 6, 2037

Gemini (May 21 - June 20)
You will experience Divine Timing Challenge Season Four during this time.
October 16, 2036, to February 11, 2037
July 6, 2037, to September 5, 2039

Cancer (June 21 - July 22)
You will experience Divine Timing Challenge Season Four during this time.
September 5, 2039, to November 11, 2041
June 21, 2042, to July 14, 2042

Leo (July 23 - August 22)
You will experience Divine Timing Challenge Season Four during this time.
July 14, 2042, to February 21, 2044
March 25, 2044, to October 31, 2044

Virgo (August 23 - September 22)
You will experience Divine Timing Challenge Season Four during this time.
February 21, 2044, to March 25, 2044
October 31, 2044, to January 24, 2047
July 10, 2047, to October 22, 2047

Libra (September 23 - October 22)
You will experience Divine Timing Challenge Season Four during this time.
December 19, 2017, to March 21, 2020
July 1, 2020, to December 17, 2020
January 24, 2047, to July 10, 2047

October 22, 2047, to January 21, 2050

Scorpio (October 23 - November 21)
You will experience Divine Timing Challenge Season Four during this time.
March 21, 2020, to July 1, 2020
December 17, 2020, to March 7, 2023

Sagittarius (November 22 - December 21)
You will experience Divine Timing Challenge Season Four during this time.
March 7, 2023, to May 24, 2025
September 1, 2025, to February 13, 2026

The ache for home lives in all of us, the safe place where we can go as we are and not be questioned.

Maya Angelou

Navigate the Challenges
Divine Timing Challenge - Season Four

When you are in Divine Timing Challenge Four, this transit and season can make your life feel unstable. Challenge Four represents our sense of home, family, parents, real estate, and our very anchor in life. During this transit, it may seem there's an issue no matter where you live. I recall when my sister had this transit, no matter where she lived there was an issue, either with the place or a neighbor.

She moved to a beautiful loft, but they ended up not giving her the one she originally reserved. The place had construction going on so there were always leaks and dust everywhere in my sister's unit. Let me start by saying this was supposed to be a very affluent and luxury loft, so definitely not expected.

My sister is extremely allergic to mold and dust. We then found a window of opportunity of another unit coming available in the building which seemed better and still had the high loft ceilings, exposed brick, and lots of light but without construction issues. When she moved in, she had a neighbor who was super harassing, always yelling violently at his spouse and even threatening my sister, so no rest for the weary. I recall when my mom and my uncle were experiencing Divine Challenge Season Four, my grandmother (their mother) was diagnosed with advanced kidney disease.

My uncle took care of my grandmother tirelessly. My mother would go there often, and my grandmother would stay with us on many occasions as well. They were concerned for my grandmother's well-being and health during this time. The care she received was excellent, and she ended up living many years past her initial diagnosis. She loved living with my uncle. It was a true blessing. We were so grateful for the extra time as my grandmother was simply a magical, beautiful woman who we dearly love and miss.

Instead of worrying or being concerned for your parents' health and well-being or having the responsibility of being caretaker or caregiver, this challenge season may manifest as having issues getting along with your parents at this time.

Your parents may bring stress and anxiety to your life during this challenge season. You may feel your relationship is not going well or even toxic. This is a good time to be there for your parents by spending time where the wind is at your back which is wherever you are experiencing blessings during this season.

Your divine season of blessings can be found in the Nurture the Blessing section of this book. Feel free to highlight aspects and focuses so you can start to train yourself to focus on the right area of life at the right time – that would be the blessings.

This season can bring up a concern over a home matter, a real estate matter, a living situation issue, or your parents, in essence, what makes us feel secure in life. However, when we are going through the Divine Timing Nurture the Blessing Season Four, everything is different.

This season can make us feel unstable because it represents, in essence, home and family, and that is often what makes us feel stable. We need a place to go home that is peaceful so we can rest and heal our hearts, souls, and minds after a long day.

It's important to note that we always have an area of challenge, and we always have an area of blessing that we are experiencing simultaneously. It's unfortunate that we as human beings have been wired to nurture the challenge and starve the blessing. It is my hope we can learn to do the opposite as it will change your very life.

With this transit of Divine Challenge Season Four, the best way to make it through is to find the blessings you are going through at that time. For instance, during a season of challenge, you may have blessings in your house of spirituality, Nurture the Blessings – Divine Timing Season Twelve. Season Twelve is a time of introspection, spirituality, and journeying within. You are blessed by hidden forces, divine angels, and practices like yoga, shamanistic journeying, meditation. They can all be sources of joy for you while you're going through this challenge, your focus in that area of blessing, for example. To find out where your blessings are during this challenging season, be sure to check out the Nurture the Blessings section and look for the timing cycles for your sun sign and ascendant or rising sign. Challenge Season Four can be tough. However, by focusing on your blessing and utilizing that blessing season to navigate this challenge, you will be successful.

Lessons You Are Learning Divine Timing Challenge – Season Four

- Focus on the blessings for security.
- One or both of your parents may need your assistance at this time.
- It is not a good time to purchase a home or move – plan to move before or after this cycle.
- If you need to move, consult with an astrologer as to dates that will work with your chart, or wait for this divine challenge season to pass.
- Be as loving as you can to your parents; even if they are stressing you, give your best.
- It's best not to start renovations at this time or hire any contractors. If you must, get referrals and do background checks.
- Check in often on your family and be a source of love and light.
- See situations as a divine being looking down from heaven. Take yourself out of the situation and view from higher ground.
- Remember the law of everything is love; give it to yourself.
- Remember you can be your own source of security. Simply take the time to build new foundations that serve you well.

<u>Navigate the Challenges</u>

Divine Timing Challenge – Season Five

Your romantic life and children are challenged.

Divine Time You Are in Now

Sagittarius (November 22 - December 21)
You will experience Divine Timing Challenge Season Five during this time.
May 24, 2025, to September 1, 2025
February 13, 2026, to April 12, 2028

Capricorn (December 22 - January 19)
You will experience Divine Timing Challenge Season Five during this time.
April 12, 2028, to May 31, 2030

Aquarius (January 20 - February 18)
You will experience Divine Timing Challenge Season Five during this time.
May 31, 2030, to July 13, 2032

Pisces (February 19 - March 20)
You will experience Divine Timing Challenge Season Five during this time.
July 13, 2032, to August 26, 2034
February 15, 2035, to May 11, 2035

Aries (March 21st - April 19)
You will experience Divine Timing Challenge Season Five during this time.
August 26, 2034, to February 15, 2035

May 11, 2035, to October 16, 2036
February 11, 2037, to July 6, 2037

Taurus (April 20 - May 20)
You will experience Divine Timing Challenge Season Five this time.

October 16, 2036, to February 11, 2037
July 6, 2037, to September 5, 2039

Gemini (May 21 - June 20)
You will experience Divine Timing Challenge Season Five during this time.

September 5, 2039, to November 11, 2041
June 21, 2042, to July 14, 2042

Cancer (June 21 - July 22)
You will experience Divine Timing Challenge Season Five during this time.

July 14, 2042, to February 21, 2044
March 25, 2044, to October 31, 2044

Leo (July 23 - August 22)
You will experience Divine Timing Challenge Season Five during this time.

February 21, 2044, to March 25, 2044
October 31, 2044, to January 24, 2047
July 10, 2047, to October 22, 2047

Virgo (August 23 - September 22)
You will experience Divine Timing Challenge Season Five during this time.

December 19, 2017, to March 21, 2020
July 1, 2020, to December 17, 2020
January 24, 2047, to July 10, 2047
October 22, 2047, to January 21, 2050

Libra (September 23 - October 22)
You will experience Divine Timing Challenge Season Five during this time.
March 21, 2020, to July 1, 2020
December 17, 2020, to March 7, 2023

Scorpio (October 23 - November 21)
You will experience Divine Timing Challenge Season Five during this time.
March 7, 2023, to May 24, 2025
September 1, 2025, to February 13, 2026

Navigate the Challenges
Divine Timing Challenge - Season Five

When you are in the Divine Timing Challenge Season Five, life can seem like it's lacking love, romance, and fun. You will also potentially have a challenge at this time in this season with adopting a child or getting pregnant. It's important to note that this is a season, and the wonderful thing about seasons is that they change.

At this time, you may instead be concerned for your child, or your child may be a stressor for you. I had a dear friend enduring this Divine Timing Challenge Season, which is Saturn transiting her house of children, and she suffered with extreme postpartum disorder after giving birth. She greatly loved her children and loves them dearly! She is one of the best young mothers I know. However, during this challenging time, her children were a great stressor to her emotionally, mentally, physically, and spiritually. Yet, after experiencing Divine Timing Challenge Season Five, she started a practice to help other mothers suffering from postpartum depression in silence.

I recall going through this challenge and the sense of lack I had in my love life. It seemed to last forever. Everyone I dated had issues with commitment, were not ready for a relationship, or just were not a good fit for my life. When experiencing Divine Challenge Season Five, your sense of fun, love, and romance is challenged. It seems like everyone you date is the wrong fit, or there are no dates to be found if you're looking for love. The great thing to note is that this season does not last forever. However, this season is fraught with pain as it can make life feel lackluster. It's hard to let loose and have fun. It seems like your childlike sense of wonder is gone, and all you desire is more fun, love, and romance in your life.

This is again how Teacher Saturn shines a light on what we are lacking so we realize its meaning when we have it. My husband and I both went through challenges in relationships before we met one another, as everyone does. We have a mature understanding that we are blessed to have each other, even when we get into spats and disagreements. This is how Saturn teaches. By going through these moments of pain and isolation when we are blessed with true love, it's easier to recognize it, and it increases its value.

Love can be such an amazing thing when you're with the right person. When you're with the wrong person, romantic love can be toxic. No one wants to experience Challenge Five as it's a real Debbie Downer. It's a time when play can seem nonexistent, and our life feels null and void of true joy. During this time, it is imperative that we refocus our lives and refocus our intention on nurturing the current blessings.

The current blessings can be found in the Nurture the Blessings section of this book. Look for your corresponding sun sign and rising or ascendant sign. Be sure to focus on that blessing area of life during these challenges and approach all challenges from your placement of blessings.

You may be concerned about your child's performance in school. Perhaps they are being bullied or just going through some rough years adjusting due to Divine Timing Challenge Season Five. I suggest checking in on your children often for physical, emotional, and spiritual well-being. And another option, assistance can come from the area of life in which you are experiencing blessings. For example, perhaps during the same Challenge Season Five, your Nurture the Blessings are occurring in the sector of life of your parents and family. You can ask your parents to be a source of confidence or be a confidant for your child. You can encourage your child to spend time with your parents or your trusted siblings who can be an adult voice of reason that will be a blessing to you and your child during this season. Where there is a will, there is always a way. We just have to know how to navigate the challenges, starve them, and nurture and feed the blessings.

Lessons You Are Learning Divine Timing Challenge – Season Five

- True love is like a rare diamond.
- Unconditional love for our children.
- Be vigilant in caring for your children; infants all the way to your adult children may need your love and guidance more at this time.
- When you find love, cherish it.
- There is a time and season for everything. Be present in the moment when you are having fun moments as these times are precious.
- Play and fun are essential for joy in life; treasure these things.
- Self-love is a gift. Nurture it
- There are many types of love besides romantic love, and they are all valuable.
- Friendships are always valuable, particularly in the absence of romantic love.
- Never settle; it is better to be alone than in a bad romantic relationship.
- Love is a gift, but it takes two.

Navigate the Challenges

Divine Timing Challenge – Season Six

Your Work Life and Sense of Overall Health and Well-Being Is Being Challenged.

Divine Time You Are in Now

Scorpio (October 23 - November 21)
You will experience Divine Timing Challenge Season Six during this time.
May 24, 2025, to September 1, 2025
February 13, 2026, to April 12, 2028

Sagittarius (November 22 - December 21)
You will experience Divine Timing Challenge Season Six during this time.
April 12, 2028, to May 31, 2030

Capricorn (December 22 - January 19)
You will experience Divine Timing Challenge Season Six during this time.
May 31, 2030, to July 13, 2032

Aquarius (January 20 - February 18)
You will experience Divine Timing Challenge Season Six during this time.
July 13, 2032, to August 26, 2034
February 15, 2035, to May 11, 2035

Pisces (February 19 - March 20)
You will experience Divine Timing Challenge Season Six during this time.

August 26, 2034, to February 15, 2035

May 11, 2035, to October 16, 2036

February 11, 2037, to July 6, 2037

Aries (March 21st - April 19)
You will experience Divine Timing Challenge Season Six during this time.

October 16, 2036, to February 11, 2037

July 6, 2037, to September 5, 2039

Taurus (April 20 - May 20)
You will experience Divine Timing Challenge Season Six during this time.

September 5, 2039, to November 11, 2041

June 21, 2042, to July 14, 2042

Gemini (May 21 - June 20)
You will experience Divine Timing Challenge Season Six during this time.

July 14, 2042, to February 21, 2044

March 25, 2044, to October 31, 2044

Cancer (June 21 - July 22)
You will experience Divine Timing Challenge Season Six during this time.

February 21, 2044, to March 25, 2044

October 31, 2044, to January 24, 2047

July 10, 2047, to October 22, 2047

Leo (July 23 - August 22)
You will experience Divine Timing Challenge Season Six during this time.

December 19, 2017, to March 21, 2020

July 1, 2020, to December 17, 2020

January 24, 2047, to July 10, 2047
October 22, 2047, to January 21, 2050

Virgo (August 23 - September 22)
You will experience Divine Timing Challenge Season Six during this time.
March 21, 2020, to July 1, 2020
December 17, 2020, to March 7, 2023

Libra (September 23 - October 22)
You will experience Divine Timing Challenge Season Six during this time.
March 7, 2023, to May 24, 2025
September 1, 2025, to February 13, 2026

Navigate the Challenges
Divine Timing Challenge –
Season Six

When you are experiencing Divine Timing Challenge Season Six, life can be very stressful in regard to work, daily routines, health, and well-being.

You may have a job that does not align with your goals or bring you joy. You may have a boss who micromanages you, or you may have issues with colleagues and co-workers. It's a time when the daily stresses of life can seem overwhelming. It's also a time when a bad work situation can actually make you feel sick, affecting your overall sense of well-being.

If you're in a job you love, it can be hard to hire the right people. A trusted colleague or co-worker you depend on might leave. A new hire, if you're in management, may become a stressor. You may also be concerned about your health and well-being. It could be minor issues cropping up or major ones. It's imperative that before this season occurs, to nurture your health and well-being. It's equally important that you follow a healthy regimen during this season and do all you can to nurture your physical and mental well-being for that matter.

If you find you are in this season, there will be opportune times where teacher Saturn may be playing well with the other planets. This is where a good astrological session can come in handy. It's important to note times of opportunity that you can utilize during this challenge season to help improve your vitality, health, and well-being.

Divine Timing Challenge Season Six does not necessarily always bring up a health issue. It could be issues with getting things done and/or feeling like you are overwhelmed and overstressed with work which can cause a feeling of being out of sorts or lack of well-being. I suggest that to combat these feelings, really pay attention to your body – listen to your higher self. When you feel it's time to go to the doctor, don't delay. Research and apply healthy measures in integrative or holistic medicine to keep your mind, body, and spirit feeling well.

If you are in a toxic work situation, look for opportune times to look for new work. Perhaps it's time to take a leap of faith toward your true goals and dreams. The best indication is to look to where your blessings are coming in and nurture that source. Sometimes, a toxic work situation leads us to our greatest blessings because with a comfortable work situation, we may never leave or make our dreams come true. It's important to note that while you have this challenge, there is always an area of blessing happening simultaneously. We always want to shift our focus counterintuitively away from the challenge and toward what is blessing us.

If you can focus on these blessings, it is from this area of life that you would find healing at this time and help. To find what blessing time you are in, turn to the Nurture the Blessing section of this book and find the corresponding dates for your sun sign and ascendant or rising sign.

Lessons You Are Learning Divine Timing Challenge – Season Six

- The value of a great work environment
- How to create a work environment of value
- The importance of a daily work routine for your health and well-being
- Prevention is the best medicine.
- The body is resilient, and if you give it what it needs to heal, you can heal.
- The power of natural herbs and holistic methods – in essence, the gifts of the universe toward natural healing and well-being
- Traditional and nontraditional healing methods
- A message you may have for others or a gift you learn from your ailment and then healing
- The preciousness of health and wellness
- Kindness and appreciation toward our physical bodies

<u>Navigate the Challenges</u>

Divine Timing Challenge – Season Seven

Your Relationship With Others Is Being Challenged.

Divine Time You Are in Now

Libra (September 23 - October 22)
You will experience Divine Timing Challenge Season Seven during this time.
May 24, 2025, to September 1, 2025
February 13, 2026, to April 12, 2028

Scorpio (October 23 - November 21)
You will experience Divine Timing Challenge Season Seven during this time.
April 12, 2028, to May 31, 2030

Sagittarius (November 22 - December 21)
You will experience Divine Timing Challenge Season Seven during this time.
May 31, 2030, to July 13, 2032

Capricorn (December 22 - January 19)
You will experience Divine Timing Challenge Season Seven during this time.
July 13, 2032, to August 26, 2034
February 15, 2035, to May 11, 2035

Aquarius (January 20 - February 18)
You will experience Divine Timing Challenge Season Seven during this time.
August 26, 2034, to February 15, 2035

May 11, 2035, to October 16, 2036
February 11, 2037, to July 6, 2037

Pisces (February 19 - March 20)
You will experience Divine Timing Challenge Season Seven during this time.
October 16, 2036, to February 11, 2037
July 6, 2037, to September 5, 2039

Aries (March 21st - April 19)
You will experience Divine Timing Challenge Season Seven during this time.
September 5, 2039, to November 11, 2041
June 21, 2042, to July 14, 2042

Taurus (April 20 - May 20)
You will experience Divine Timing Challenge Season Seven during this time.
July 14, 2042, to February 21, 2044
March 25, 2044, to October 31, 2044

Gemini (May 21 - June 20)
You will experience Divine Timing Challenge Season Seven during this time.
February 21, 2044, to March 25, 2044
October 31, 2044, to January 24, 2047
July 10, 2047, to October 22, 2047

Cancer (June 21 - July 22)
You will experience Divine Timing Challenge Season Seven during this time.
December 19, 2017, to March 21, 2020
July 1, 2020, to December 17, 2020
January 24, 2047, to July 10, 2047
October 22, 2047, to January 21, 2050

Leo (July 23 - August 22)
You will experience Divine Timing Challenge Season Seven during this time.
March 21, 2020, to July 1, 2020
December 17, 2020, to March 7, 2023

Virgo (August 23 - September 22)
You will experience Divine Timing Challenge Season Seven during this time.
March 7, 2023, to May 24, 2025
September 1, 2025, to February 13, 2026

Navigate the Challenges
Divine Timing Challenge – Season Seven

When you are experiencing this divine time of challenge, Divine Timing Challenge Season Seven, it is in my opinion one of the most challenging of all divine timing challenge seasons taught by Teacher Saturn. This timing focuses on the sector of life ruling partnerships, marriage, business partnerships, open enemies, and any formal partnership or lack thereof.

This particular challenge and divine time can make you feel as if the world is completely against you. It feels like nothing is working out. During this season, you may be concerned about the well-being of a marriage partner, or you may be experiencing difficulty during this time in a marriage or other committed relationship.

We all go through different seasons, and experiencing difficulty does not mean it's the end, by any means. It does communicate the fact that there must be adjustments and changes within yourself and/or within the other person – in essence, your partnership.

It's a time you must take a stance for yourself. You have to be your own champion, and this is specifically a time you must devote all of your energy to mental, emotional, and physical well-being. I advise working with a coach and counselor during this transition and taking steps toward body, spirit, and mind wellness. It's important to fill your life with things that bring you small doses of joy, whether that's utilizing something small like your favorite lavender soap while taking a bath or shower. Designing your space with your favorite plants to make your home feel more peaceful and any way you can ease the pressures of this challenge is advised.

This is a time when it is imperative that you nurture your body, spirit, soul, and mind. This is a time when you must choose yourself.

If you are in a marriage, you may decide at this time to completely change your life to create a more supportive environment for your partner and your life together. Choosing your own wellness can be simply making yourself a priority, deciding to change things in your life that are no longer working for your highest good.

During this challenging time, you will want to spend as much time as possible in the area of life in which you are experiencing blessings or good fortune. You will want to place your intention and energy there in a particularly strong way while nurturing your emotional, mental, and spiritual well-being at the same time. It's hard for me to understand how such a difficult challenge could be allowed by the Universe, but everything we experience helps us become more of who we are meant to be while experiencing the Earth in our chosen life experience.

This challenge, which can affect you up to three times within a lifetime, is simply to help you have a sense of self-love and self-reliance in spite of everything and the ability to rise to the occasion of any challenge, learning to how to be self-reliant and have self-trust and self-love, even when it appears the whole world is against you. This Divine Timing Challenge Seven, which is part of Saturn's parenting style of a challenge-based reality, should also help you get in touch with your higher self and your spiritual self as you will need the miracles of heaven. The miracles of grace and gratitude and a divine love for yourself. You will need all there is to help you hone into the beauty of life and come out better for it on the other side. Remember to nurture the current Divine timing blessing season you are in and seek hope and help there. Focus on divine self-care and self-love and know this is a season, so it will change.

Lessons You Are Learning Divine Timing Challenge – Season Seven

- You may feel lack of partnership
- Desire for a partnership
- Lessons about partnership
- What works in a partnership and what does not work
- Qualities you need in a future husband or wife
- Desirable qualities in a business partnership
- Developing a sense of self-love
- Finding healthy ways to fend off loneliness

<u>Navigate the Challenges</u>

Divine Timing Challenge – Season Eight

Your Financial Resourcefulness and Intimacy Are Being Challenged.

Divine Time You Are in Now

Virgo (August 23 - September 22)
You will experience Divine Timing Challenge Season Eight during this time.
May 24, 2025, to September 1, 2025
February 13, 2026, to April 12, 2028

Libra (September 23 - October 22)
You will experience Divine Timing Challenge Season Eight during this time.
April 12, 2028, to May 31, 2030

Scorpio (October 23 - November 21)
You will experience Divine Timing Challenge Season Eight during this time.
May 31, 2030, to July 13, 2032

Sagittarius (November 22 - December 21)
You will experience Divine Timing Challenge Season Eight during this time.
July 13, 2032, to August 26, 2034
February 15, 2035, to May 11, 2035

Capricorn (December 22 - January 19)
You will experience Divine Timing Challenge Season Eight during this time.

August 26, 2034, to February 15, 2035
May 11, 2035, to October 16, 2036
February 11, 2037, to July 6, 2037

Aquarius (January 20 - February 18)
You will experience Divine Timing Challenge Season Eight during this time.
October 16, 2036, to February 11, 2037
July 6, 2037, to September 5, 2039

Pisces (February 19 - March 20)
You will experience Divine Timing Challenge Season Eight during this time.
September 5, 2039, to November 11, 2041
June 21, 2042, to July 14, 2042

Aries (March 21st - April 19)
You will experience Divine Timing Challenge Season Eight during this time.
July 14, 2042, to February 21, 2044
March 25, 2044, to October 31, 2044

Taurus (April 20 - May 20)
You will experience Divine Timing Challenge Season Eight during this time.
February 21, 2044, to March 25, 2044
October 31, 2044, to January 24, 2047
July 10, 2047, to October 22, 2047

Gemini (May 21 - June 20)
You will experience Divine Timing Challenge Season Eight during this time.
December 19, 2017, to March 21, 2020
July 1, 2020, to December 17, 2020

January 24, 2047, to July 10, 2047
October 22, 2047, to January 21, 2050

Cancer (June 21 - July 22)

You will experience Divine Timing Challenge Season Eight during this time.
March 21, 2020, to July 1, 2020
December 17, 2020, to March 7, 2023

Leo (July 23 - August 22)

You will experience Divine Timing Challenge Season Eight during this time.
March 7, 2023, to May 24, 2025
September 1, 2025, to February 13, 2026

Navigate the Challenges
Divine Timing Challenge – Season Eight

When you are navigating Divine Timing Challenge Season Eight, it can be a time of financial stress and even tax your well-being. Divine Timing Challenge Season Eight is all about resources, taxes, sales, venture capital, credit, creditors, inheritances, other people's money, loans, mortgages, and sexual and reproductive health.

This lesson is all about respect for your resources. This is a time when you also want to guard your credit and protect against any sort of identity theft. If you are awaiting an inheritance, there could be a delay because it is contested or some other issue.

It is a time where it might be more difficult to get funding for things such as a mortgage or a business loan. If you are in sales, commissions may be slow, and sales may slow down as well. It's a time of limitations in regard to getting funding for projects, properties, or any sort of funding that is not generated from your earned income. Sometimes, this challenge shows up during a divorce when people are dividing property. I want to note that this challenge does not mean you'll be getting a divorce; it's just one circumstance that sometimes occurs during this challenge.

We have all heard the stories of couples being married for 50+years. During that span of time, a couple can go through Divine Timing Challenge Eight at least twice. So, this challenge in no way denotes a split. I think we see a split occur in some charts that did not handle Divine Timing Challenge Seven well, which is when you are experiencing challenges in a committed relationship or marriage.

Divine Timing Challenge Season Eight can also restrict sexual activity. This challenge within medical astrology can lead to erectile dysfunction or issues with the prostate. It can also lead to menstrual or reproductive issues for women. During Divine Challenge Eight, it's also a time to be wise with sexual habits. With planet teacher Saturn reigning over this lesson, Saturn wants us to always be responsible. Be sure to make wise decisions with intimate connections and be responsible. Your body is a divine temple; know your value and worth.

This challenge holds all of the taboo subjects we've been speaking about here – the fun stuff like death, rebirth, taxes, and taboo topics like sex. However, we have not really spoken about death or rebirth within the realm of this divine challenge. Divine Challenge Season Eight also represents the phoenix rising from the ashes.

Many of us in our own lives have lived so many lives in one life it seems like we die and then are reborn several times in one life. These miniature rebirths and deaths can be triggered by a divorce, a marriage, a new job, a new business, moving cross country, growing up with our family, building our own family, or being president of a company then losing everything in the stock market and working for someone else. These miniature deaths and rebirths are all a part of this sector of life in Divine Challenge Season Eight.

The best way to navigate this divine timing challenge is to be vigilant about making wise choices and decisions regarding money, debt, and investing – in essence, resources available to you. Be wise when taking on new loans and debts and develop a true appreciation of the resources within our grasp to create a life with meaning.

Lessons You Are Learning Divine Timing Challenge – Season Eight

- Be vigilant about protecting your resources and assets. Remember one of your greatest assets is your body.
- Enroll in an identity theft protection site like LifeLock or myfico.com.
- Be wise with taking on any new loans or credit and get ahead on credit card bills.
- Devise a proven strategy for investing in your future.
- Nurture Your Blessings – Go to the proceeding chapter Nurture Your Blessings to locate where your blessings are at this time, and focus on that. Remember whatever we nurture grows stronger.
- Women, make regular visits to your OB/GYN; men, take care of your prostate health.
- Make a financial plan and budget and stick to it.
- Be wise with making new sexual connections, and always be sexually responsible.
- It may be time for a rebirth, and that may be uncomfortable, but if you are to rise as the phoenix, become your best version of yourself.
- Focus on your divine timing blessing season!

<u>Navigate the Challenges</u>

Divine Timing Challenge – Season Nine

Your Ideals, Knowledge, and Beliefs Are Being Challenged.

Divine Time You Are in Now

Leo (July 23 - August 22)
You will experience Divine Timing Challenge Season Nine during this time.
May 24, 2025, to September 1, 2025
February 13, 2026, to April 12, 2028

Virgo (August 23 - September 22)
You will experience Divine Timing Challenge Season Nine during this time.
April 12, 2028, to May 31, 2030

Libra (September 23 - October 22)
You will experience Divine Timing Challenge Season Nine during this time.
May 31, 2030, to July 13, 2032

Scorpio (October 23 - November 21)
You will experience Divine Timing Challenge Season Nine during this time.
July 13, 2032, to August 26, 2034
February 15, 2035, to May 11, 2035

Sagittarius (November 22 - December 21)
You will experience Divine Timing Challenge Season Nine during this time.

August 26, 2034, to February 15, 2035

May 11, 2035, to October 16, 2036

February 11, 2037, to July 6, 2037

Capricorn (December 22 - January 19)

You will experience Divine Timing Challenge Season Nine during this time.

October 16, 2036, to February 11, 2037

July 6, 2037, to September 5, 2039

Aquarius (January 20 - February 18)

You will experience Divine Timing Challenge Season Nine during this time.

September 5, 2039, to November 11, 2041

June 21, 2042, to July 14, 2042

Pisces (February 19 - March 20)

You will experience Divine Timing Challenge Season Nine during this time.

July 14, 2042, to February 21, 2044

March 25, 2044, to October 31, 2044

Aries (March 21st - April 19)

You will experience Divine Timing Challenge Season Nine during this time.

February 21, 2044, to March 25, 2044

October 31, 2044, to January 24, 2047

July 10, 2047, to October 22, 2047

Taurus (April 20 - May 20)

You will experience Divine Timing Challenge Season Nine during this time.

December 19, 2017, to March 21, 2020

July 1, 2020, to December 17, 2020

January 24, 2047, to July 10, 2047
October 22, 2047, to January 21, 2050

Gemini (May 21 - June 20)
You will experience Divine Timing Challenge Season Nine during this time.
March 21, 2020, to July 1, 2020
December 17, 2020, to March 7, 2023

Cancer (June 21 - July 22)
You will experience Divine Timing Challenge Season Nine during this time.
March 7, 2023, to May 24, 2025
September 1, 2025, to February 13, 2026

Navigate the Challenges
Divine Timing Challenge – Season Nine

When you're experiencing Divine Timing Challenge Season Nine, it's all about growth, learning, exploration, international travel, publishing, religion, and higher education.

It's about exploring big ideas and different cultures while traveling and learning internationally. As they say, to be well-traveled is a goal in higher learning. As we learn through travel while accepting and exploring other cultures, we learn through exploring other beliefs and religions that are different from our own. We learn through reading books, writing books, and teaching others. Education can be traditional like exploring a degree or an advanced degree at an institution for higher learning like a college or university. Learning can also be non-traditional like exploring Europe, backpacking in the Amazon Forest, or visiting the Galapagos islands.

Someone well-traveled tends to come off as cultured, more accepting, and with a high degree of intelligence, just as those immigrants who ventured to relocate to the United States, Europe, Dubai, or a culture different than their own to experience a completely different perspective on life. Divine Timing Challenge Season nine is one of the softer divine timing lessons. However, with Master Teacher Saturn teaching Divine Timing Challenge Nine, it can be an experience of great focus with some delays and challenges, of course.

When we are going through a divine timing challenge, it is part of the human condition that our mind naturally harps on the challenge, as that is where we are currently experiencing difficulty, delays, and or stress. The great thing about this divine season is that it can give you more focus if you are pursuing higher education, and it can give you great focus if you are pursuing any of the forms of education that we have mentioned in this section. However, if you are traveling, it can cause delays and other stressors like traveling internationally and awaiting a work visa or green card. If you're in school, you may have very demanding professors, and the work may be much more challenging and difficult than you originally perceived.

If you're working at getting a book published at this time, you will have the focus to get it done. However, getting with your desired publisher or agent may be more challenging than you anticipated. This challenge will mainly cause delays and require your complete structure toward your goal for success.

If you're pursuing traditional education at a college or university during this time, you will need to give 100% focus to your education, completing assignments on time and following all proper methods and procedures to be successful.

If you are attempting to relocate overseas, this effort might be delayed until Divine Timing Challenge Nine is completed. Look to the first page of this section to find the periods of time when you're in Divine Timing Challenge Nine and also look to the Nurture the Blessing section to define advantageous times to relocate that would be when you're in Divine Timing Blessing Season Nine.

Divine Timing Challenge Season Nine also governs over religion. If you are religious, you may have issues with clergy at this time or other church-goers. This may also be a time when you completely decide that religion does not work for you, and you may question ideas and religious concepts that were previously your foundation. You may also become completely consumed with religion if you have previously been non-religious. You'll start to question the deeper meanings of life, and religion may be very attractive to you during this time. It's important to note that religion and spirituality are in two separate sectors of life as we look at these things from an astrological perspective. Divine Timing Season Nine speaks to religion, and Divine Timing Season Twelve governs spirituality. They are both very different, but both are very necessary in the divine lessons of life.

Lessons You Are Learning Divine Timing Challenge - Season Nine

- Learn about and embrace new cultures. However, if you're traveling, be sure to check out the reviews. And rather than traveling solo, travel with trusted dear friends and/or family members, if possible. Be smart with travel at this time. Listen to your gut.

- If enrolling in a university program for a bachelor's or master's degree or a PhD, be prepared for hard work and also for potentially very tough professors. You can do it! You'll have the focus, and it will be a challenge.

- If traveling overseas, be sure to double check any travel restrictions, and be sure your passport is up to date. Make sure you have a passport that does not expire during your trip.

- If relocating overseas or to another country, be sure you give ample time to receive your work visa or green card. Divine Challenge Nine can cause all sorts of delays and mishaps with getting international paperwork approved.

- When studying religion or getting involved in religion or a new church, take a balanced approach.

- It's a wonderful time to read and soak up as much knowledge as possible. Listen to audiobooks, take a master class, study a new language, etc.

- In any of the above-mentioned topics, realize there may be delays and extra challenges as this is Divine Timing Challenge Nine.

- Learn where your current blessings are coming in by examining the Nurture the Blessings chapter. Pursue all of your interests in this area by nurturing your current blessings.

<u>Navigate the Challenges</u>

Divine Timing Challenge – Season Ten

Your Professional Standing in This World Is Being Challenged.

Divine Time You Are in Now

Cancer (June 21 - July 22)
You will experience Divine Timing Challenge Season Ten during this time.
May 24, 2025, to September 1, 2025
February 13, 2026, to April 12, 2028

Leo (July 23 - August 22)
You will experience Divine Timing Challenge Season Ten during this time.
April 12, 2028, to May 31, 2030

Virgo (August 23 - September 22)
You will experience Divine Timing Challenge Season Ten during this time.
May 31, 2030, to July 13, 2032

Libra (September 23 - October 22)
You will experience Divine Timing Challenge Season Ten during this time.
July 13, 2032, to August 26, 2034
February 15, 2035, to May 11, 2035

Scorpio (October 23 - November 21)
You will experience Divine Timing Challenge Season Ten during this time.

August 26, 2034, to February 15, 2035
May 11, 2035, to October 16, 2036
February 11, 2037, to July 6, 2037

Sagittarius (November 22 - December 21)
You will experience Divine Timing Challenge Season Ten during this time.

October 16, 2036, to February 11, 2037
July 6, 2037, to September 5, 2039

Capricorn (December 22 - January 19)
You will experience Divine Timing Challenge Season Ten during this time.

September 5, 2039, to November 11, 2041
June 21, 2042, to July 14, 2042

Aquarius (January 20 - February 18)
You will experience Divine Timing Challenge Season Ten during this time.

July 14, 2042, to February 21, 2044
March 25, 2044, to October 31, 2044

Pisces (February 19 - March 20)
You will experience Divine Timing Challenge Season Ten during this time.

February 21, 2044, to March 25, 2044
October 31, 2044, to January 24, 2047
July 10, 2047, to October 22, 2047

Aries (March 21st - April 19)
You will experience Divine Timing Challenge Season Ten during this time.

December 19, 2017, to March 21, 2020
July 1, 2020, to December 17, 2020

January 24, 2047, to July 10, 2047
October 22, 2047, to January 21, 2050

Taurus (April 20 - May 20)
You will experience Divine Timing Challenge Season Ten during this time.
March 21, 2020, to July 1, 2020
December 17, 2020, to March 7, 2023

Gemini (May 21 - June 20)
You will experience Divine Timing Challenge Season Ten during this time.
March 7, 2023, to May 24, 2025
September 1, 2025, to February 13, 2026

Navigate the Challenges
Divine Timing Challenge - Season Ten

When you are in Divine Challenge Season Ten, it may seem that everything you do career wise takes extreme effort. If you get a promotion at a current job, demands can be so taxing that you may crave simpler times. Divine Challenge Season Ten is all about our career and our professional standing in this world.

Remember the divine challenges in this chapter are all taught by Teacher Saturn. Saturn, as a teacher, respects a disciplined approach, responsibility, and following all the proper measures and procedures to create success.

Teacher Saturn never wants us to skip a step. If we skip steps and don't follow procedures or are irresponsible, Saturn will slap us down and make us start over. When you encounter Divine Challenge Season Ten, it is imperative that you follow every rule, policy, and procedure in your industry and in your life to protect your reputation and standing in the world. Your standing in the world can encompass your career accomplishments, your career dreams and goals, and how you are viewed in your industry and the greater world. When you encounter this challenge, it is time to step up to the plate and give your best. Teacher Saturn allows no room for error, and of course as human beings, that is sometimes impossible.

That is why this challenge is so challenging. However, during this challenge season, approach every task with integrity and take the high road, even when others take the low road. If you work for an employer, you may have a higher up who makes work feel miserable or challenging. You may have a colleague who is threatened by your success and may try to throw obstacles along your path. At this time, it is imperative to just do your best while learning this lesson of Saturn.

The lesson of Divine Timing Challenge Season Ten is all journeys and careers require adjustments and have ups and downs.

It asks the question, if this is your chosen profession, are you willing to experience the ups and downs of your industry? As I have witnessed throughout life, the commitments corporate jobs require are equal to pursuing your true purpose and passions in life. Neither path will be easy, and each path will have its own sets of responsibilities, setbacks, and opportunities for growth and success. However, you must choose your poison or choose your tincture of blessing.

Sometimes, working a traditional job you're good at and getting paid for it can be very important for you to be able to sustain while pursuing other goals in an economy where you feel it's not time to go out on your own and pursue your passions. So, there is no harm in being wise and calculated about your moves to pursue your passions.

However, it is noted that it takes just as much sacrifice to succeed at something that is not your passion while working toward someone else's passion as it does to succeed at your own. So, if you'll have to go through the strife and the challenges anyway, then you might as well pursue your true purpose in your career.

Another lesson of this challenge is we are constantly going through a rebirth in this life, and that includes our career path. We need to remain agile to change at all times. Never get fixed to one path, and realize there's more than one path to obtaining your desired career success and delivery of your purpose on this Earth.

Lessons You Are Learning Divine Timing Challenge - Season Ten

- Follow all proper processes and procedures in your current career for success.
- If something is your responsibility and it does not succeed, take responsibility. This will make you shine during this time.
- Make sure you have all the proper certifications and necessary tools to succeed in your career.
- If you want to make a career change during this time, make sure you are prepared and have done the groundwork.
- There are good managers, and there are bad managers who are of no consequence to you, at least you're not married to them. When you go to work, you're there to do a job; do not let bad management get you emotional. You are there to succeed.
- Check out the Nurture the Blessings chapter in this book. Find out where your blessings are currently, and nurture that source of energy.
- Meditate daily on what you want to manifest in your life. Write it down, and learn what it will take to achieve your goal. Also, be honest with yourself as to if you are willing to take the necessary steps to be successful in that chosen field.
- Be honest with yourself as to your performance at work or in your chosen career field; if you need to make improvements, make them.
- Attitude is everything, in spite of even a toxic work or business environment. Be resilient with your attitude, and be

your best version of yourself, even in the presence of your enemies.

- Remember this is a season, and the great thing about seasons is they change.

"Character cannot be developed in ease and quiet. Only through experience of trial and suffering can the soul be strengthened, ambition inspired, and success achieved."

– Helen Keller

<u>Navigate the Challenges</u>

Divine Timing Challenge – Season Eleven

Your Friends, Friendships, and Social Groups Are Being Challenged.

Divine Time You Are in Now

Gemini (May 21 - June 20)
You will experience Divine Timing Challenge Season Eleven during this time.
May 24, 2025, to September 1, 2025
February 13, 2026, to April 12, 2028

Cancer (June 21 - July 22)
You will experience Divine Timing Challenge Season Eleven during this time.
April 12, 2028, to May 31, 2030

Leo (July 23 - August 22)
You will experience Divine Timing Challenge Season Eleven during this time.
May 31, 2030, to July 13, 2032

Virgo (August 23 - September 22)
You will experience Divine Timing Challenge Season Eleven during this time.
July 13, 2032, to August 26, 2034
February 15, 2035, to May 11, 2035

Libra (September 23 - October 22)
You will experience Divine Timing Challenge Season Eleven during this time.

August 26, 2034, to February 15, 2035
May 11, 2035, to October 16, 2036
February 11, 2037, to July 6, 2037

Scorpio (October 23 - November 21)
You will experience Divine Timing Challenge Season Eleven during this time.
October 16, 2036, to February 11, 2037
July 6, 2037, to September 5, 2039

Sagittarius (November 22 - December 21)
You will experience Divine Timing Challenge Season Eleven during this time.
September 5, 2039, to November 11, 2041
June 21, 2042, to July 14, 2042

Capricorn (December 22 - January 19)
You will experience Divine Timing Challenge Season Eleven during this time.
July 14, 2042, to February 21, 2044
March 25, 2044, to October 31, 2044

Aquarius (January 20 - February 18)
You will experience Divine Timing Challenge Season Eleven during this time.
February 21, 2044, to March 25, 2044
October 31, 2044, to January 24, 2047
July 10, 2047, to October 22, 2047

Pisces (February 19 - March 20)
You will experience Divine Timing Challenge Season Eleven during this time.
December 19, 2017, to March 21, 2020
July 1, 2020, to December 17, 2020

January 24, 2047, to July 10, 2047
October 22, 2047, to January 21, 2050

Aries (March 21st - April 19)
You will experience Divine Timing Challenge Season Eleven during this time.
March 21, 2020, to July 1, 2020
December 17, 2020, to March 7, 2023

Taurus (April 20 - May 20)
You will experience Divine Timing Challenge Season Eleven during this time.
March 7, 2023, to May 24, 2025
September 1, 2025, to February 13, 2026

Navigate the Challenges
Divine Timing Challenge – Season Eleven

In Divine Timing Challenge Season Eleven, we are learning about friendship, a sense of humanity, and social networking. During this challenge, you may find it more difficult to make friends. You may have just relocated to a new city and are finding that making friends is something you hugely want, but it is challenging. If you have a group of friends (they say we have very few true friends in life), this Divine Timing Challenge Eleven will show you any cracks in your friendships and give you a tried-and-true lesson of who your true friends are.

During this time, friends you make may be opportunistic or just not in alignment with what you want to create in your life. If you are working on a humanitarian cause or serve on a board, you may find your board assignment to be unfulfilling and stressful.

If you have dear friends, you see often, they may suddenly move away or be preoccupied with other obligations. As you seek friendships, it appears most people are just acquaintances, and your long-standing friendships may encounter some challenges and misunderstandings as well.

Divine Challenge Season Eleven is teaching us about the value of friendships, the value of community, and the value of having a non-romantic social life. Divine Challenge Eleven also governs over social media platforms and the internet.

This is not a good time to date online or meet strangers via Facebook or any other social media channel. I highly recommend that if you want to try online dating, you wait until Divine Challenge Eleven is over, then look to the place where you're currently experiencing blessings in the Nurture the Blessings chapter. Your current

Divine Blessing Season is the area you should focus on if you want to meet acquaintances or a potential love interest.

If you must do social media posts for your business during this time, hire a social media manager. That is the most assured way to achieve success in social media during this time. During this challenging time, you may have a sense of loneliness. You may also be worried about a dear friend's well-being and want to be there for him or her. That is something I'm sure your dear friend would appreciate if they're having a rough time.

This divine challenge season teaches us the value of friendships, the value of humanity, and the value of having a sense of community. This divine challenge season also teaches us traits that we need in our friendships and traits we should avoid as we choose our circle of friends. As you experience the ends and outs of this time, friends that survive Divine Challenge Eleven will stand the test of time.

Lessons You Are Learning Divine Timing Challenge – Season Eleven

- Choose friends that inspire you by their lives.
- Avoid getting into rifts on social media.
- Avoid any online dating apps until challenge season eleven is over.
- Look to the Nurture the Blessings section of this book to nurture where your blessings are coming in at this time.
- You may be concerned for a friend's well-being, and you'll want to be there for your friend.
- You may have issues with a nonprofit board or another board membership and need to decide if it's worth investing your time there.
- Make sure friendships are adding good to your life, and get rid of any toxic friendships.
- Be your own best friend at this time. Take yourself for spa dates, and perhaps adopt a dog at this time.
- Be aware and meditate on the traits you want in your friend-ships and the types of friendships you want so you may attract these types of friends to yourself in the future.
- It's good to forgive and forget any friends' mistakes but also note if these are the type of friends you want in your life. Sometimes, people we meet are meant to be our friends, and sometimes, they are meant to be acquaintances. Know the difference.

<u>Navigate the Challenges</u>

Divine Timing Challenge – Season Twelve

Your Approaches to Spiritual and Mental Well-Being Are Being Challenged.

Divine Time You Are in Now

Taurus (April 20 - May 20)
You will experience Divine Timing Challenge Season Twelve during this time.
May 24, 2025, to September 1, 2025
February 13, 2026, to April 12, 2028

Gemini (May 21 - June 20)
You will experience Divine Timing Challenge Season Twelve during this time.
April 12, 2028, to May 31, 2030

Cancer (June 21 - July 22)
You will experience Divine Timing Challenge Season Twelve during this time.
May 31, 2030, to July 13, 2032

Leo (July 23 - August 22)
You will experience Divine Timing Challenge Season Twelve during this time.
July 13, 2032, to August 26, 2034
February 15, 2035, to May 11, 2035

Virgo (August 23 - September 22)
You will experience Divine Timing Challenge Season Twelve during this time.

August 26, 2034, to February 15, 2035

May 11, 2035, to October 16, 2036

February 11, 2037, to July 6, 2037

Libra (September 23 - October 22)

You will experience Divine Timing Challenge Season Twelve during this time.

October 16, 2036, to February 11, 2037

July 6, 2037, to September 5, 2039

Scorpio (October 23 - November 21)

You will experience Divine Timing Challenge Season Twelve during this time.

September 5, 2039, to November 11, 2041

June 21, 2042, to July 14, 2042

Sagittarius (November 22 - December 21)

You will experience Divine Timing Challenge Season Twelve during this time.

July 14, 2042, to February 21, 2044

March 25, 2044, to October 31, 2044

Capricorn (December 22 - January 19)

You will experience Divine Timing Challenge Season Twelve during this time.

February 21, 2044, to March 25, 2044

October 31, 2044, to January 24, 2047

July 10, 2047, to October 22, 2047

Aquarius (January 20 - February 18)

You will experience Divine Timing Challenge Season Twelve during this time.

December 19, 2017, to March 21, 2020

July 1, 2020, to December 17, 2020

January 24, 2047, to July 10, 2047
October 22, 2047, to January 21, 2050

Pisces (February 19 - March 20)
You will experience Divine Timing Challenge Season Twelve during this time.
March 21, 2020, to July 1, 2020
December 17, 2020, to March 7, 2023

Aries (March 21st - April 19)
You will experience Divine Timing Challenge Season Twelve during this time.
March 7, 2023, to May 24, 2025
September 1, 2025, to February 13, 2026

"Religion is for people who fear hell; spirituality is for people who have been there."

— David Bowie

Navigate the Challenges
Divine Timing Challenge - Season Twelve

When experiencing Divine Timing Challenge Season Twelve, there is a yin and yang to this placement. Challenge Season Twelve encompasses wellness, spirituality, the subconscious, working alone in self-imposed isolation, holistic wellness, shamanism, spiritual gifts, intuition, and unseen forces such as spirit guides and angels. Divine Timing Challenge Season Twelve also holds secrets and events happening behind the scenes.

This challenge season can be a bit of self-imposed isolation and seeking for greater spiritual truth. This area also covers wellness, confinement, hospitals, and working focused and alone like a hermit.

With Teacher Saturn here, if you are working on a project that requires great focus, you will have focus in spades. That is on the positive note. This challenge season, also ruling the subconscious mind, may make you feel limited and potentially depressed, underappreciated, and isolated from the world. A big part of this might be self-imposed isolation.

Divine Timing Challenge Season Twelve also represents addiction and imprisonment and can point to a time of mental health issues. On the positive side of Divine Timing Challenge Season Twelve, this sector of life represents spirituality, the spirit world, and higher frequencies of living. Also represented here is art, inspiration, music, and film.

We'll start with speaking about Divine Timing Challenge Season Twelve from a spiritual perspective. An aspect of the spirit world is it is a form of protection, offering solitude and serenity from the mundane pressures of life on Earth. Not to say life on earth does not have excitement, joys, and beauty. Life on Earth is a rare gift to be treasured. However, the spirit world gives us a sense of empowerment, power, and freedom or escape from the mundane which we can access anytime through meditation or other spiritual practices. With Divine Timing Challenge Season Twelve, you may seek escapism with drugs, alcohol, or other means that are a detriment to your well-being. As we have spoken about earlier in this chapter, Challenge Twelve has a yin-and-yang effect. You can reach higher levels of consciousness through means that are healthy such as meditation, sound baths, hikes in nature, shamanism, and natural herbs and juices or through reckless means like drugs or overindulgence in alcohol.

Divine Timing Challenge Season Six is more about physical well-being, and stress is for sure in that arena. While Divine Timing Challenge Twelve affects more of our daily routines, fitness, health, and daily work, Divine Timing Challenge Season Twelve encompasses spiritual wellness that affects the body, spirit, and mind. To make the most of this time, you will want to nurture the positive elements of this placement. Also, look to the Nurture the Blessings chapter to see where your current blessings are coming in. Be sure to nurture that area of life. Find the corresponding dates of blessing cycles in that chapter for your Sun and rising sign.

If you feel like self-isolating, do that in healthy ways like reading a book and maybe even doing so alone at an inspiring coffee shop. If you love to write, it's fine to self-isolate at home, but get yourself out and about in a routine of being somewhere you love that is beautiful and will inspire you. While you may want to separate yourself completely from the world, it is not 100% healthy for you at this time. It's best, even if you desire to work alone, to work in places that inspire you as opposed to maybe working from home. In essence, you'll still be alone at your table, but you will be surrounded by beautiful art or elements that inspire you.

If you've had an issue with drug or alcohol abuse, it's a good time to seek help. Remember the divine timing challenge seasons are taught by teacher Saturn. Saturn looks at all of our methods and wants us to follow processes and procedures with no short-cuts. Certainly, use of drugs or overindulgence in alcohol is a shortcut that can lead to our detriment. It's a form of escapism. It is helpful on our path and for our utmost and highest good if we utilize our spiritual tools to reach higher ground in a spiritual way.

It's a wonderful time to take account of your emotional, mental, and spiritual well-being and enroll in a wellness program or just use your own daily regimen in this regard, perhaps incorporating tai chi, yoga, Pilates, hiking, paddle boarding, or simply taking walks. It's an excellent time to seek out help with a therapist for any past or enduring trauma or to gain understanding over your thoughts and feelings. You can also look to working with a life coach to help you to achieve your wellness goals.

Research natural herbs or work with an herbalist if dealing with anxiety or stress. If going to a therapist who believes in holistic approaches or integrative medicine, make sure you let them know if you are on any current antidepressants. I, for one, personally appreciate natural supplements and herbs as they have generally no side effects. And if they do have a side effect, it's something that helps the body as opposed to hurts the body. Ask your doctor about inositol (B complex) which works wonders for OCD and ADHD. For calming herbs, you can look into Passionflower, Ashwagandha, Holy Basil, and Saint John's Wort. There are many herbalists in Chinese medicine, Ayurvedic medicine, and in Western medicine that can help. There are also medical doctors who are not only MDs and/or psychiatric doctors but also certified and/or knowledgeable about integrative medicine.

If you can find a doctor such as this, it is recommended. However, the most important thing to do is to seek help and know your body; try to use the most natural means to heal first, and then if you must be prescribed something for mental wellness, look up the side effects and be aware of what you're taking before you put it in your body. Ask questions of your physician, and keep a daily journal about how you are feeling on the medication.

Divine Timing Challenge Season Twelve also encompasses the arts such as film, visual art, and music. If you are in these fields, they will be in extreme focus for you. Make sure you follow all of the proper processes and procedures to have a successful career in these fields, so you are rewarded at the end of this divine timing challenge. Also, be sure to surround yourself with inspiring music around your home and with art, if possible.

Divine Timing Challenge Season Twelve can be a time that revolutionizes your life in a positive way or can completely destroy you. It is up to you.

Lessons You Are Learning Divine Timing Challenge – Season Twelve

- Spirituality versus escapism
- Define what spirituality means to you.
- Start a wellness plan, and put it into action.
- Avoid self-isolating too much.
- Seek help from a therapist.
- If in the arts, film, or music, be up for the challenge. Create your masterpiece; however, be sure to follow all processes and procedures that are needed in your field to be successful.
- Play inspiring music throughout your home; engulf your home with plants.
- Cleanse your home space with sage often.
- Start a meditation practice.
- Seek out a life coach.
- Explore concepts that add to your health and your overall wellness, including body, spirit, soul, and mind.
- Be careful with any addiction. If you have an addiction, now is the time to seek help.
- Be careful with prescription drugs, antidepressants, etc. If you've been prescribed them by a doctor, it may be important to see someone who's actually a psychiatrist who understands the side effects of such prescriptions. Be the master of your own health and well-being.

INDEX

The Simplicity of
The Power of Divine Timing

Through simplicity, life's most complex problems can be resolved. *The Power of Divine Timing* is a technique that is really quite simple. Anyone can utilize this technique and knowledge to create happier, more fulfilling lives.

This technique can be utilized by someone who knows nothing about astrology and by the most advanced astrologer, if you are open minded. While simple, the techniques in this book are counterintuitive. They are so simple, in fact, that they can actually change your life when applied.

It doesn't matter how much we know about astrology, including progressions, transits, eclipses, houses, elements of past, present, and future, or philosophies, if we can't use the data to make our lives more fulfilling and utilize the knowledge to manifest our greatest intentions.

That's why I love the techniques taught in this book, because if you practice them daily, you can change your life in such dynamic ways.

In this book, we utilize different terminology than traditional western astrology. While our astrological data is based on astrological cycles, houses, transits, etc., this book makes the complex simple so we can focus on one thing — nurturing our current blessings and starving our challenges.

215

It is this simplicity that takes complex topics down to one focus point and peels away all unnecessary layers for a profound understanding of the message the stars & planets teach; the message is that living in the moment requires focusing on where current good is coming in so we can get to the next level in life we desire to manifest. This is why in *The Power of Divine Timing*, we call transits "divine timing seasons" because seasons change. This simplistic method creates desired outcomes by simply focusing on and nurturing the correct source of energy at the correct time. Through adjusting your thought process to the methods described in this book, you can create the success of actually having more balance in life, being more joyful, and creating the financial success, career success, and success in love and marriage that you desire to manifest in the here and now.

"In simplicity is found the solutions to life's most complex problems..."

— Joy Yascone–Elms

The Power of Divine Timing Index

The Power of Divine Timing™ — The technique that locates your specific, personal Universal blessings and challenges in real time and simply teaches you how to starve your challenges and nurture and grow your blessings!

Astrological Fingerprint – Your unique and divine attributes attributed at birth, your birth or natal chart.

The Teachers – The planets teaching us each a different lesson in life.

Master Teachers – Teacher Planets Jupiter and Saturn. These planets make the most impact in teaching us lessons annually. Master Teacher Jupiter takes 12 years to travel the entire Zodiac, and Saturn takes 28-29 years.

The Wind at Your Back – This comes from The Irish Blessing, describing a time of blessing.

Nurture the Blessings – There are 12 divine blessing seasons taught by Master Teacher Jupiter. When we focus on these times of opportunity, we increase our ability to manifest.

House – House is an astrological term utilized in astrology that relates to a certain sector of life. A house in astrology basically refers to an area of life. There are 12 "houses" or sectors of life in astrology.

Transit – A transit represents the movement of a planet through the various constellations, houses, or points. A transit can relate to your birth chart or simply the current movements of the planets. This book looks at the transits of Saturn and Jupiter as seasons.

Divine Timing Seasons – Divine timing blessing seasons are governed by Master Teacher Jupiter. Challenge seasons are governed by Master Teacher Saturn. In *The Power of Divine Timing*, we look at transits or movements of Jupiter and Saturn impacting your natal chart or astrological fingerprint as divine timing seasons.

Divine Timing Blessing Seasons – Advantageous times of blessing and good fortune when planet Master Teacher Jupiter is transiting or traveling through a sector of life. In traditional astrology, this is called a "house" for the purposes of manifesting within divine timing. We refer to it as a season.

The Twelve Blessing Seasons — The 12 blessing seasons are taught by benevolent planet and Master Teacher Jupiter. These blessing seasons each last a duration of 12 months. You will experience the same blessing season every 12 years.

Divine Timing Blessing Season One – Divine Timing Blessing Season One is the wonderful divine timing season when Jupiter, planet and teacher of benevolence and good fortune, "transits" your first house of self. The "house" of self is different for each individual chart and is based on your Sun and/or rising sign. In *The Power of Divine Timing*, we look at transits of Jupiter and Saturn as divine timing seasons. To learn more about Divine Timing Blessing Season One, go to that chapter.

Divine Timing Blessing Season Two – Divine Timing Blessing Season Two focuses on delivering immense blessings to you financially as Jupiter sets up Divine Timing Blessing Season Two in your second "house" (or sector) of earned income, governing what we value and financial opportunities through income we earn. To learn more about Divine Timing Blessing Season Two, go to that chapter.

Divine Timing Blessing Season Three – Divine Timing Blessing Season Three focuses on helping us with communication, relationships with siblings, and negotiation of and receiving contracts. During this season, focus on healing sibling relationships, writing in any form including music, improving communication skills, and/or taking a public speaking class. When you experience Blessing Season Three, Jupiter is moving through or in "transit" to your third house governing all these areas. To learn more about Divine Timing Blessing Season Three, go to that chapter.

Divine Timing Blessing Season Four – Divine Timing Blessing Season Four is a time of blessing in real estate matters, family blessings, parents, and, in essence, anything that makes your life feel more secure. Divine Timing Blessing Season Four is a "transit" of Teacher Jupiter to the fourth "house" governing home. To learn more about Divine Timing Blessing Season Four, go to that chapter.

Divine Timing Blessing Season Five– Divine Timing Blessing Season Five is all about romantic love, creativity, children, having a childlike sense of wonder, play and procreation, and pregnancy. Divine Timing Blessing Season Five is a "transit" of Teacher Jupiter to the fifth "house" governing all of these areas of life. To learn more about Divine Timing Blessing Season Five, go to that chapter.

Divine Timing Blessing Season Six– Divine Timing Blessing Season Six is all about work, daily routines, fitness, and health. Divine Timing Blessing Season Six is a "transit" of Teacher Jupiter to the sixth "house" governing over health, fitness, daily routines, and work. To learn more about Divine Timing Blessing Season Six, go to that chapter.

Divine Timing Blessing Season Seven – This season is all about marriage, any form of partnership, business, or in love and marriage. Also, attorneys, agents, allies, and opposition from known enemies. All of these areas are blessed in your favor during this season. It's one of the best indications of marriage or engagement! Divine Timing Season Seven is a "transit" of Teacher Jupiter to the seventh "house" governing partnership and marriage. To learn more about Divine Timing Blessing Season Seven, go to that chapter.

Divine Timing Blessing Season Eight – Divine Timing Blessing Season Eight is all about funding big dreams! Venture capital, mortgages, investments, investors, credit, debts, inheritances, rebirth, death, taxes, and sex are all in this divine blessing season. This is a season of great ability to fund a dream. Divine Timing Blessing Season Eight is a "transit" of Teacher Jupiter to the Eighth "house" governing these areas of life. To learn more about Divine Timing Blessing Season Eight, go to that chapter.

Divine Timing Blessing Season Nine – This is a time when you are blessed with good fortune in international relations, international or long-distance travel, opportunities in publishing and broadcasting, and higher education such as a degree. Divine Timing Blessing Season Nine is a "transit" of Teacher Jupiter to the ninth "house" governing these areas of life. To learn more about Divine Timing Blessing Season Nine, go to that chapter.

Divine Timing Blessing Season Ten – Divine Timing Blessing Season Ten governs over your career and professional standing. During this divine timing blessing season, you can expect divine blessings in your career. Divine Timing Blessing Season Ten is a "transit" of Teacher Jupiter to the tenth "house," career status and professional standing in the world. To learn more about Divine Timing Blessing Season Ten, go to that chapter.

Divine Timing Blessing Season Eleven – Divine Timing Blessing Season Eleven is a "transit" of Teacher Jupiter to your eleventh "house" and is all about blessings in friendships, humanitarian causes, socializing, social media, technology, and the web or internet, astrology, and the interconnected web of divine consciousness. Divine Timing Blessing Season Eleven is a "transit" of Teacher Jupiter to the eleventh "house" governing these areas of life. To learn more about Divine Timing Blessing Season Eleven, go to that chapter.

Divine Timing Blessing Season Twelve – Divine Timing Blessing Season Twelve is a "transit" of Teacher Jupiter to your twelfth "house" and governs over body, spirit, and mind, wellness, spirituality, divinity, film, music, and the arts. Hospitals and imprisonment also here and working in isolation. Also, escapism, drugs and alcohol, therapy, healing, and all alternative healing modalities. Shamanism, spirit guides, clairvoyance, and all spiritual gifts are in this season as well. During this blessing season, experience the wellness of body, spirit, and mind. Embark on an artistic and spiritual journey. Divine Timing Blessing Season Twelve is a "transit" of Teacher Jupiter to the twelfth "house" governing these areas of life. To learn more about Divine Timing Blessing Season Twelve, go to that chapter.

The Twelve Challenge Seasons — The Divine Timing Challenge Seasons are governed by teacher Saturn. These seasons last in duration of 2½ -3 years. There are 12 divine timing challenge seasons. To learn when you will experience this divine timing challenge, go to that chapter. Also, check out what divine timing blessing season you are in in the Nurture the Blessings chapters.

Divine Timing Challenge Season One – Divine Timing Challenge Season One focuses challenges on your sense of self. This season is taught by Teacher Saturn as Saturn transits your house of self. The "House of Self'" is different for each individual chart and is based on your Sun and/or rising sign.

To learn when you will experience Divine Timing Challenge Season One, go to that chapter. Also, check out what divine timing blessing season you are in in the Nurture the Blessings chapters.

Divine Timing Challenge Season Two – Divine Timing Challenge Season Two focuses on challenges to your finances through earned income. Teacher Saturn gives you a trial-by-fire lesson plan in Divine Timing Challenge Season Two in your second "house" or sector of earned income governing over what we value and financial opportunities through income we earn. To learn when you will experience Divine Timing Challenge Season Two, go to that chapter. Also, check out what divine timing blessing season you are in in the Nurture the Blessings chapters.

Divine Timing Challenge Season Three – Divine Timing Challenge Season Three focuses on challenging or limiting us in communication, relationships with siblings, and negotiation. During this season, sibling relationships may be challenged, or a sibling may need your help. Writing in any form, including music, communication skills, and public speaking, may endure challenges. To learn when you will experience Divine Timing Challenge Season Three, go to that chapter. Also, check out what divine timing blessing season you are in in the Nurture the Blessings chapters.

Divine Timing Challenge Season Four – Divine Timing Challenge Season Four is a time of blessing in real estate matters, family, parents, and, in essence, anything that makes your life feel more secure. Divine Timing Challenge Season Four is a "transit" of Teacher Saturn to the fourth "house" governing over these areas of life. To learn when you will experience this divine timing challenge, go to that chapter. Also, check out what divine timing blessing season you are in in the Nurture the Blessings chapters.

Divine Timing Challenge Season Five – Divine Timing Challenge Season Five is all about romantic love, creativity, children, having a childlike sense of wonder, play, and procreation. Divine Timing Challenge Season Five, taught by Teacher Saturn, is a "transit" of Saturn to the fifth house therefore bringing challenges to the fifth "house" which governs the above-mentioned sectors of life. To learn when you will experience Divine Timing Challenge Season Five, go to that chapter. Also, check out what divine timing blessing season you are in in the Nurture the Blessings chapters.

Divine Timing Challenge Season Six – Divine Timing Challenge Season Six is all about work, daily routines, fitness, and health. This is a time when Teacher Saturn transits through your sixth "house" and delivers lessons through challenges in these areas of life. To learn when you will experience Divine Timing Challenge Season Six, go to that chapter. Also, check out what divine timing blessing season you are in in the Nurture the Blessings chapters.

Divine Timing Challenge Season Seven – Divine Timing Challenge Season Seven is all about marriage, any form of partnership, business, or in love and marriage. Also, attorneys, agents, allies, and opposition from known enemies. All of these areas are potential areas of challenge during this season. To learn when you will experience Divine Timing Challenge Season Seven, go to that chapter. Also, check out what divine timing blessing season you are in in the Nurture the Blessings chapters.

Divine Timing Challenge Season Eight – This divine timing challenge season is all about being challenged in financing from other resources besides income you earn. This includes venture capital, mortgages, investments, investors, credit, debts, inheritances, taxes, and scx. To lcarn when you will experience Divine Timing Challenge Eight, go to that chapter. Also, check out what divine timing blessing season you are in in the Nurture the Blessings chapters.

Divine Timing Challenge Season Nine – This is a time when you are challenged in international relations, international or long-distance travel, opportunities in publishing and broadcasting, and higher education such as a degree. To learn when you will experience Divine Timing Challenge Season Nine, go to that chapter. Also, check out what divine timing blessing season you are in in the Nurture the Blessings chapters.

Divine Timing Challenge Season Ten – Divine Timing Challenge Season Ten governs over your career and professional standing. During this divine timing challenge season, you can expect divine challenges in your career to achieve advancement. Divine Timing Challenge Season Ten is a "transit" of Teacher Saturn to the tenth "house" governing career. To learn when you will experience Divine Timing Challenge Season Ten, go to that chapter. Also, check out what divine timing blessing season you are in in the Nurture the Blessings chapters.

Divine Timing Challenge Season Eleven – Divine Timing Challenge Season Eleven is all about challenges in friendships, humanitarian causes, socializing, social media, technology, and the web or internet, astrology, and the interconnected web of divine consciousness. You may feel isolated as Teacher Saturn "transits" your eleventh "house," and it's not a good time to meet someone through online dating. To learn when you will experience Divine Timing Challenge Season Eleven, go to that chapter. Also, check out what divine timing blessing season you are in in the Nurture the Blessings chapters.

Divine Timing Challenge Season Twelve – In Divine Timing Challenge Season Twelve, Teacher Saturn is in "transit" to the twelfth "house" governing body, spirit, and mind wellness, spirituality, divinity, film, music, and the arts. Hospitals and imprisonment also here and working in isolation. Also, escapism, drugs, and alcohol, therapy, healing, and all alternative healing modalities. Shamanism, spirit guides, clairvoyance, and all spiritual gifts are in this season as well. During this challenge season, resist escapism into drugs and alcohol and spend as much time as possible in whatever blessing season you are in. To learn when you will experience this divine timing challenge go to that chapter. Also, check out what divine timing blessing season you are in in the Nurture the Blessings chapters.

Tracking Jupiter's Movements Through the Signs – Jupiter Is a Master Teacher and Governs Blessings

Jupiter will transit these star signs on the dates below.

For your Nurture the Blessings–Divine Timing Blessing Season dates or Divine Timing–Navigate the Challenges Season dates, go to those chapters.

Jupiter in Aries
May 10, 2022, to October 28, 2022
December 20, 2022, to May 16, 2023
April 21, 2034, to April 29, 2035

Jupiter in Taurus
May 16, 2023, to May 25, 2024
April 29, 2035, to May 9, 2036
April 13, 2047, to April 22, 2048

Jupiter in Gemini
May 25, 2024, to June 9, 2025
May 9, 2036, to May 23, 2037
April 22, 2048, to September 23, 2048
November 12, 2048, to May 5, 2049

Jupiter in Cancer
June 9, 2025, to June 30, 2026
May 23, 2037, to June 12, 2038

September 23, 2048, to November 12, 2048
May 5, 2049, to September 27, 2049

Jupiter in Leo
June 30, 2026, to July 26, 2027
June 12, 2038, to November 16, 2038
January 16, 2039, to July 7, 2039

Jupiter in Virgo
July 26, 2027, to August 24, 2028
November 16, 2038, to January 16, 2039
July 7, 2039, to December 12, 2039
February 20, 2040, to August 5, 2040

Jupiter in Libra
August 24, 2028, to September 24, 2029
December 12, 2039, to February 20, 2040
August 5, 2040, to January 11, 2041
March 20, 2041, to September 5, 2041

Jupiter in Scorpio
September 24, 2029, to October 22, 2030
January 11, 2041, to March 20, 2041
September 5, 2041, to February 8, 2042
April 24, 2042, to October 4, 2042

Jupiter in Sagittarius
October 22, 2030, to November 15, 2031
February 8, 2042, to April 24, 2042
October 4, 2043, to June 9, 2043

Jupiter in Capricorn
November 15, 2031, to April 11, 2032
June 26, 2032, to November 29, 2032
March 1, 2043, to June 9, 2043

October 26, 2043, to March 15, 2044
August 9, 2044, to November 4, 2044

Jupiter in Aquarius

December 19, 2020, to May 13, 2021
July 28, 2021, to December 28, 2021
April 11, 2032, to June 26, 2032
November 29, 2032, to April 14, 2033
September 12, 2033, to December 1, 2033
March 15, 2044, to August 9, 2044

Jupiter in Pisces

May 13, 2021, to July 28, 2021
December 28, 2021, to May 10, 2022
October 28, 2022, to December 20, 2022
April 14, 2033, to September 12, 2033
December 1, 2033, to April 21, 2034

Tracking Saturn's Movements Through the Signs – Saturn Is a Master Teacher and Governs Challenges

The Transits of Teacher Saturn

For your Nurture the Blessings–Divine Timing Blessing Season dates or Divine Timing–Navigate the Challenges Season dates, go to those chapters.

Saturn in Aries
May 24, 2025, to September 1, 2025
February 13, 2026, to April 12, 2028

Saturn in Taurus
April 12, 2028, to May 31, 2030

Saturn in Gemini
May 31, 2030, to July 13, 2032

Saturn in Cancer
July 13, 2032, to August 26, 2034
February 15, 2035, to May 11, 2035

Saturn in Leo
August 26, 2034, to February 15, 2035
May 11, 2035, to October 16, 2036
February 11, 2037, to July 6, 2037

Saturn in Virgo
October 16, 2036, to February 11, 2037
July 6, 2037, to September 5, 2039

Saturn in Libra
September 5, 2039, to November 11, 2041
June 21, 2042, to July 14, 2042

Saturn in Scorpio
July 14, 2042, to February 21, 2044
March 25, 2044, to October 31, 2044

Saturn in Sagittarius
February 21, 2044, to March 25, 2044
October 31, 2044, to January 24, 2047
July 10, 2047, to October 22, 2047

Saturn in Capricorn
December 19, 2017, to March 21, 2020
July 1, 2020, to December 17, 2020
January 24, 2047, to July 10, 2047
October 22, 2047, to January 21, 2050

Saturn in Aquarius
March 21, 2020, to July 1, 2020
December 17, 2020, to March 7, 2023

Saturn in Pisces
March 7, 2023, to May 24, 2025
September 1, 2025, to February 13, 2026

References

David Bowie. (n.d.). AZQuotes.com. Retrieved August 21, 2022, from AZQuotes.com Web site: https://www.azquotes.com/author/1736-David_Bowie

DeMers, J. (2014, November 3). 51 quotes to inspire success in your life and business. Inc.com. Retrieved August 19, 2022, from https://www.inc.com/jayson-demers/51-quotes-to-inspire-success-in-your-life-and-business.html

Flatow, I. (2013, May 17). Resetting the theory of Time. NPR. Retrieved August 19, 2022, from https://www.npr.org/2013/05/17/184775924/resetting-the-theory-of-time#:~:text=Albert%20Einstein%20once%20wrote%3A%20People,that%20true%20reality%20is%20timeless

King James Bible. (2020). King James Bible Online. https://www.kingjames-bibleonline.org

Morgan, J.P. (n.d.). AZQuotes.com. Retrieved August 19, 2022, from AZQuotes.com Web site: https://www.azquotes.com/quote/578814

National Day of Prayer: Irish prayers and blessings for your friends and family. IrishCentral.com. (2021, July 6). Retrieved August 19, 2022, from https://www.irishcentral.com/roots/irish-prayers-blessings

Ziglar, Zig. (n.d.). AZQuotes.com. Retrieved August 19, 2022, from AZQuotes.com Web site: https://www.azquotes.com/quote/826893

Maya Angelou." AZQuotes.com. Wind and Fly LTD, 2022. 23 August 2022. https://www.azquotes.com/quote/8502

Joy Yascone-Elms

Joy Yascone Elms MA is an astrologist and astrological intuitive that has coached hundreds of clients to success in career, love, marriage, and business, utilizing *The Power of Divine Timing™ technique.* *The Power of Divine Timing™ is* a program that aligns you with the divine timing of the Universe to manifest your greatest intentions and desires—all based on astrological timing. After attending graduate school and earning a Master's in Holistic Health from Georgian Court University — Joy founded the Power of Divine Timing technique through her astrological coaching practice, which was offered at historic and notable Wainwright House in Rye, New York.

Joy started to see her clients' lives change rapidly. "We just rewired their thinking, thoughtfully examined their birth chart, and reconciled where the blessings were coming in utilizing astrological data, so we could nurture the correct source of energy at the correct time. The problem is that this is, in fact, very counterintuitive. If you have a problem, you think on it until you solve it, right? It works in math. However, in life and in utilizing *The Power of Divine Timing*, our goal is to shift intention away from what is challenging us and toward what is blessing our lives", states author and founder of *The Power of Divine Timing*™ Joy Yascone-Elms.

Joy's methodology is based on the premise that whatever you feed grows stronger. Place intention on the challenges, they grow stronger; and place intention on the blessings, and they grow as well! Joy utilizes astrological data to locate these time patterns of opportunity for clients and readers.

Joy has helped clients utilizing astrological data for over 15 years, earning her Master of Arts in Holistic Health studies; focusing much of her studies on holistic counseling techniques and ideas on energy, intention, and manifestation. While in New York, Joy gained first-hand experience with the technique she founded, The Power of Divine Timing ™, to nurture the correct source of energy at the right time—which led her to meet the man who would become her husband, in tune with Universal alignment. Joy writes the monthly astrology column for Sophisticated Living magazine, "Sophisticated Stars", and regularly writes astrology features for other respected magazines.

Joy also has a notable background in the intuitive arts and is a gifted composer, known for her work in film and television and for the film score "The Battle of Ypres". The Battle of Ypres is a 1925 feature film about World War I, filmed in 1925 with original footage. Joy believes in the connection of all things and that music and astrology are linked through divine frequency. Joy creates music as she does everything else, intuitively.

If you would like the opportunity to learn about The Power of Divine Timing coaching program or to learn more about Joy's upcoming appearances, please visit www.thepowerofdivinetiming.com.

Made in the USA
Columbia, SC
23 November 2022

71947377R00137